THE PALACE OF VERSAILLES

MUSÉES ET MONUMENTS DE FRANCE

GENERAL EDITOR : PIERRE LEMOINE
PUBLISHED IN COLLABORATION WITH THE RÉUNION DES MUSÉES NATIONAUX
AND THE FONDATION PARIBAS

THE PALACE OF VERSAILLES

THE NATIONAL MUSEUM OF THE PALACES OF VERSAILLES AND TRIANON

PIERRE LEMOINE

Inspecteur Général honoraire des Musées de France

ⓜ

ÉDITIONS DE LA RÉUNION DES MUSÉES NATIONAUX

This volume, the third in the series *Musées et Monuments de France*, has been made possible through the concerted efforts of the Fondation Paribas and the Réunion des musées nationaux.

This initiative reflects the desire of Paribas to be associated with the presentation of our universal cultural heritage to the French public.

Patronage has long been part of the Paribas tradition. Wishing to contribute to a fuller integration of the business world into its cultural, scientific and social environment, Paribas has for many years now worked on an international scale to encourage scientific innovation, conservation of cultural heritage and artistic creation.

This project became firmly established with the creation of the Fondation Paribas early in 1984. In addition to dealing with social issues the Fondation has done its utmost, particularly in its support of youth projects, to promote scientific and technical research and to encourage cultural and artistic expression.

Cover:
LOUIS XIV RECEIVES THE DODGE OF GENOA IN THE GALLERY OF MIRRORS AT VERSAILLES, ON MAY 15th, 1685
Frontispiece:
LOUIS XIV by Lorenzo Bernini in 1665

© Éditions de la Réunion des musées nationaux, 1987
    10, rue de l'Abbaye, 75006 Paris

© 1987 MUSÉES ET MONUMENTS DE FRANCE PARIS

I.S.B.N.: 2-7118-2-135-8 (English)
I.S.B.N.: 2-7118-2-134-X (français)

CONTENTS

INTRODUCTION
ORIGINS 7
THE PALACE OF LOUIS XIII 8
LOUIS XIV'S FIRST BUILDING PROJECT 9
THE NEW PALACE 13
THE EXTENSION TO THE PALACE 17
THE CAPITAL OF THE KINGDOM 28
18th CENTURY CULTURAL ALTERATIONS 30
TRIANON 32
THE NATIONAL MUSEUM 34

THE STATE APARTMENTS 39

THE GRAND GALLERY OR GALLERY OF MIRRORS 57

THE ROYAL CHAPEL 65

THE KING'S APARTMENT 69

THE KING'S PRIVATE APARTMENT 89

THE QUEEN'S APARTMENT 93

THE APARTMENTS OF THE DAUPHIN, THE DAUPHINE, AND THE MESDAMES DE FRANCE 103

THE ROYAL OPERA HOUSE 119

THE GARDENS 123

THE TRIANON 133

THE LITTLE TRIANON 145

THE GREATER STABLES 153

The Palace of Versailles, circa 1668 – This
painting by Pierre Patel clearly shows how
the palace looked after Louis XIV completed his first bout of works in 1662: the
circular esplanade with its obelisks, the
forecourt bordered by the new outhouses
and Louis XIII's original palace, conserved
but embellished.   To the right can be seen
Thetis' Grotto with its basin.   The gardens have already taken on their definitive
aspect and work has started on the Grand
Canal.

INTRODUCTION

The Palace of Versailles is undoubtedly the most famous royal residence in the world. Its fame and fascination are not solely due to the splendid architecture, the interior decoration and the gardens, magnificent though these are, for the attentive observer will see beyond them to the historical importance and symbolism of the palace, which put Louis XIV's creation into its true perspective.

For not only was this palace one of the most sumptuous dwellings of all time, but through its history and destiny it has become a monument to a certain coherent political outlook, and it expresses the artistic, economic and intellectual policy developed at a time when France stood unequalled in Europe.

ORIGINS

The crown lands of Versailles lie to the southwest of Paris, with the present palace standing on one of three low-lying hills overlooking a valley.

This had always been a wooded region, abounding in lakes and marshes, the last ones being drained as recently as the 18th century. Although only 20 kilometers away from Paris, the climate, even today, is harsher than in the French capital.

The origins of the name "Versailles" have been the subject of controversy for many years. The French word "versail" means a piece of land which has been weeded, so it would seem that the world's most famous palace owes its name to a piece of cleared land. The clearing must have taken place after the Treaty of Saint-Clair-sur-Epte (911 A.D.) which granted the fertile lands to the west of the river Epte to the Norman chieftain Rollon, land which was later to become Normandy. However, it was not until 1038 that the name Versailles was first to be found, on the charter of the Abbey of Saint-Pair de Chartres, in which the signature of a witness, one Hugo de Versailles appears. The founding of the seigniory and parish of Saint Julien also date to this time. The lords of Versailles were not particularly grand, but were direct vassals of the King. Their castle was built on the southern slope of the same hill on which the palace stands today, but where at the time, there stood only a windmill.

The Hundred Years' War destroyed the village and scattered the inhabitants, but as soon as peace was restored the houses were rebuilt, roads repaired and the land cultivated once more. The Sire de Soisy, now enfeoffed with this land, restored the feudal castle which was in ruins. Although this castle has long disappeared, the deed still exists and enables us to piece together a description. It was made up of a main building intercepted by a three bay side wing with two turrets standing on either side of the portal. Included in the estate were a dovecote, two courtyards, a garden, an orchard, stables, windmills, four lakes and some 80 acres of woodland, fields, copses and agricultural land.

In 1561 Marshall de Loménie de Brienne, Minister of Finance to Charles IX, became the sole lord and master of Versailles. He added considerably to the domain which grew to some 450 acres. At that time the village had a population of 500 and included a few humble inns which accomodated farmers and their cattle on their way from Normandy to Paris.

However, Brienne was murdered on the night of the Saint Bartholemew Day's Massacre on August 24, 1572, and his under-age heir sold the domain to one Albert de Gondi for the considerable sum of 35,000 livres. The Gondi family originated from Florence and had come to France with Catherine de Medicis when she came to the throne.

Protected by the Queen and her son, Charles IX, the family rapidly amassed titles, honours and wealth. The most famous member of the family is doubtless Albert de Gondi, who became Marshall of France and Duke of Retz shortly after he bought Versailles. He was not only on good terms with Henri III of France, but also with the King of Navarra, later Henri IV. The King had stayed with Brienne at Versailles in 1570, and returned to stay with Gondi from the 7th to the 9th of July, 1589. After coming to the throne of France he returned from time to time to go hunting, and on these occasions he would stay to dine with Gondi, now Duke of Retz. Indeed, Gondi's estate abounded with game and the Bourbons' inordinate love of hunting was to decide the fate of Versailles.

THE PALACE OF LOUIS XIII

Henri IV was often accompanied on these visits by the young Dauphin. He was only five years old when he first visited Versailles, but he soon became attached to the place, its wildness apparently suiting his somewhat melancholy nature. After coming to the throne as Louis XIII he would often return with a small circle of friends, which included the Duke de Saint-Simon, father of the famous memorialist. For many years, if the hunt lasted too long, Louis XIII would spend the night in the Gondi castle, or even on the straw pallet of some humble inn, until he decided to build himself a simple hunting lodge on top of the hill which overlooked the castle, surrounded by a few acres of land, where he was able to feel at home. This was built in 1623 and consisted of a main building about 24 meters long by 6 meters across, and two short side wings. Although this was altered and enlarged and soon became unrecognizable, it nevertheless formed the core around which the largest royal residence was to grow.

At first, however, the King only had five small rooms, an anteroom, a bedroom, a drawing room, dining room and dressing room. A few tapestries, some green damask or brocade-covered chairs, a billiard table, and a few chests made up the furniture. This, as Marshall de Bassompierre said to the Upper House in 1627, was indeed the "miserable Palace of Versailles, in which even a mere gentleman would take no great pride"; or, as the Venetian ambassador described it, "...a small house (the King) had made in Versailles for his leisure."

Indeed, this small house soon proved to be too small, and between 1631 and 1634 Louis XIII had it enlarged under the supervision of Philibert le Roy. Another two meters were added on the garden side and two side wings, along with two small turrets covered by stone domes which connected up the three main parts of the building at the corners. The courtyard which these now enclosed was closed off on the fourth side by a narrow terrace which rested on an arcade bordered by green and gold railings. Four pavillions were added to the corners of the main buildings and a moat was dug around the whole complex, with two bridges for access. In front of this new palace was a forecourt bordered by two buildings set aside as servants' quarters.

With its slate roof, red brick walls set off by the white stone corner pilasters and decorative framework, Louis XIII's palace was typical of

LOUIS XIII, King of France and Navarra (1601-1643), after Justus van Egmont.

the three-coloured architecture which had been fashionable at the beginning of that century, but which was already falling out of favour. In any case, it fully deserved Saint-Simon's disdainful description, when, referring to a comment of Sauval's, he called it "a little palace of cards". Transformed, embellished and then integrated into Louis XIV's vast construction, it still stands today, giving the Marble Courtyard its air of outmoded elegance.

While transformations were in progress, Louis XIII bought more land. On April 8th, 1632 he bought the seigniory of Versailles from the third son of the Duke of Retz, Jean-François de Gondi, Archbishop of Paris. On May 26th of the following year, in a ceremony attended by one thousand or so inhabitants of the small town and the local priest, the French coat of arms replaced those of the Bishop at the crossroads. The size of the palace gardens, entirely walled in, was roughly the same as today. In front of the palace lay the ornamental parterres with a small wood beyond, through which alleys were cut out to converge on a circular plot which was later to become Apollo's Basin.

The Queen and her ladies-in-waiting were only rarely admitted to this retreat, to which Louis XIII intended to retire as soon as the Dauphin came of age, in order to "devote himself to matters pertaining to his salvation."

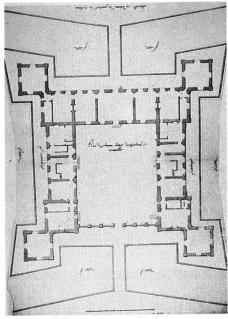

Plan of Louis XIII's palace around 1640.

However, his wish was never fulfilled, since he died prematurely in 1643 at the age of 42. The history of Versailles was then interrupted for a period of twenty years, for the new king was under five at the time and did not visit the palace before he was twelve years old, but he later got into the habit of going there to hunt from time to time, alone or with his brother. He gradually became more and more attached to his father's little hunting lodge and after he married in 1660 he began to transform it. This was just a prelude to the works which continued for practically the whole duration of his reign.

LOUIS XIV'S FIRST BUILDING PROJECT

The interior was altered as early as 1661 in order to house the King, the Queen and the Dauphin on the first floor, and the Queen Mother, the King's brother and sister-in-law on the ground floor. A staircase was built in the centre of each wing, the King's in the north wing and the Queen's in the south. These led to two symmetrical apartments, each of which included an anteroom, two drawing rooms and a bedroom, separated by a large reception room in the middle, comprising six windows, three giving onto the courtyard and three onto the garden side. None of the future transformations were to change the location of the Royal Apartments: the King would always remain on the north side and the Queen on the south.

In 1662 a wrought-iron balcony was added to the first floor along the whole of the garden side, and the painters Charles Errard and Noël Coypel redid the interior decoration. In the same year, Louis XIII's outhouses were knocked down and rebuilt to stand somewhat further apart. The new buildings housed the stables on the north side and the kitchens and pantry on the south side, around a forecourt enclosed by an iron gate bearing the arms of France. In front of this gate was a circular esplanade, the supporting walls of which ended in two obelisks at the front, and gave onto a parade ground where three grand avenues converged.

LOUIS XIV, King of France and Navarra (1638-1715), by Charles Le Brun, circa 1665.

During the next few years the King had the gardens transformed by

Plan of the palace after the 1662 works
– The forecourt is bordered by the new
outhouses, enclosing the stables on the
left, and the kitchens and pantries on the
right. The forecourt is closed by a railing
which connects two guardhouses. To the
right lies Thetis' Grotto.

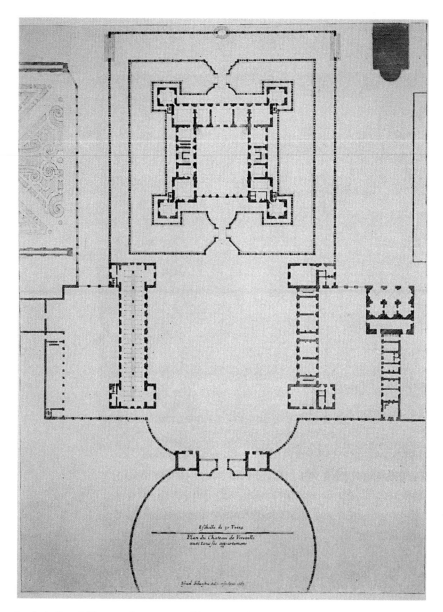

André Le Nôtre who was able to display the full extent of his
genius. He began by laying lawns and flower beds at the base of each
of the three exterior façades of the palace, taking care to vary their
shapes. On the northern side he had the land slope gently down
towards a basin, while he retained the flat surface on the southern side,
which drew up in front of a balustrade from which a lower level garden
could be seen. The two levels were connected by two sets of stairs
between which the Orangery was situated. On the western side
Le Nôtre made the steep slope more gradual, broadened the cental
path and linked up the various levels by means of ramps and steps. The
gardens were gradually taking on their definitive appearance. While
all this was going on, two small buildings were being erected which
may be counted among the most unusual of the time. The Menagerie,
at the far end of the park, was both a resting pavillion and a scientific
establishment, in which rare or exotic animals were reared and
studied. And, nearer the palace was Thetis' Grotto, a cube-shaped
edifice decorated with pebbles, shells, crystals and mother-of-pearl, and
out of which water appeared to flow from all around. Marble statues
completed the picture, notably the wonderful group of figures entitled
APOLLO WAITED ON BY THE NYMPHS OF THETIS, with which Girardon and
Regnaudin attempted to vie with the sculptors of ancient Greece and
Rome.

10

It was in these very gardens that the King gave two sumptuous entertainments, four years apart, which astounded his contemporaries and amaze us even today. In May 1664 the theme was "The Pleasures of the Enchanted Isle", and on July 18, 1668 "The Grand Royal Entertainment", undoubtedly the most extraordinary reception ever held by Louis XIV.

The southern face of the palace by Van der Meulen, circa 1665, with the first Orangery and on the right-hand side the houses of the town clustered around the parish church of Saint-Julien.

The palace from the garden side in about
1675 – This somewhat naïve painting
shows the western side of the New Palace,
built after 1669. The first-floor terrace can
be seen, with the two pavillions on either
side enclosing the last three rooms of the
King's State Apartment on the left, and the
Queen's State Apartment on the right.

THE NEW PALACE

Versailles was still only a place for entertainment, but its fame continued to grow and it became obvious that this royal residence was destined for greater things. As it stood, it was already too cramped and inconvenient and it soon became necessary to enlarge it. The King asked Louis Le Vau, his First Architect, to draw up plans for a new palace.

And now the problem arose whether or not to save the original "palace of cards". Versailles historians have always been divided on this point, but if we study the various projects put forward and analyse the chronological events of the reign, it may be possible to glean Louis XIV's real intentions.

At first the King intended to keep the "palace of cards", if only temporarily, by enveloping it on the three garden sides with the new building. This was to be built onto the back of the western part of the old palace but spaced further back on the northern and southern sides in order to include two inner courtyards. In this way the King had no need to interrupt his visits while the work was in progress, and once the new building was completed he could leave his former apartments and demolish his father's old palace. Thus the two palaces came to be known as Chateau-Vieux and Chateau-Neuf, the Old Palace and the New Palace, and only the temporary quality of the former could account for the differences in scale and style between the two ; and although both were praised at one time or another, no one ever thought to harmonize them.

But the King was not to be satisfied with a midway solution. The antiquated style of Louis XIII's palace, already out of fashion in 1634, was hardly likely to satisfy a young king who dreamed of a larger palace built after his own taste and bearing the stamp of its time. It should be noted here that the argument according to which Louis XIV preserved Louis XIII's palace out of filial piety is unfounded: he hardly knew his father. However, he did have great affection and admiration for his mother, Anne of Austria, who was made very unhappy by her husband.

The building of the new palace had hardly begun when the war with Holland broke out, and it became customary for the King to interrupt his bouts of construction work when his country was at war, so as not to divert finances. In peace time the reverse was true: he devoted all his resources to building.

The Treaty of Nijmegen signed in 1678 gave way to a ten-year truce during which the King built the Galerie des Glaces (Gallery of Mirrors), the northern and southern wings, the Grande and Petite Ecurie (Greater and Lesser Stables), the Grand Commun (outhouses) and the new Orangery. This considerable enlargement of the palace coincides, as we shall see, with Louis XIV's decision to move the court to Versailles. Meanwhile Mansart was working on the "Grand Project" of harmonizing the façades giving on to the courtyards with those on the garden side, but the war against the Grand Alliance interrupted the work yet again, up to the signing of the Treaty of Ryswick in 1697 after which the King undertook and completed the construction of the chapel, despite an outburst of renewed hostilities resulting from the Spanish succession. This was the only time works continued while the country was at war, and can be explained by the fact that by this time Louis XIV was growing old and, before he died, wanted to build a chapel worthy of a Very Christian King, in the palace which had become his main residence.

The War of Succession with Spain only came to a close in 1713, barely two years after the King's death. He therefore never saw the completion of the "Grand Project", which was inherited by his successor, who fared no better. So Versailles, like Janus, still shows its two faces to the world. It is, in fact, an unfinished building, composed of one palace fitted into another, perfectly justifying and explaining Saint-Simon's famous remark that "the beautiful and the ugly, the grandiose and the mean, were joined together."

To return to the new palace: the construction work lasted from 1668 to 1670, but the interior and exterior decoration continued for the whole of the following decade. Unlike the "palace of cards", it was built from sandstone and had flat roofs concealed behind balustrades covered with trophies and flame ornaments. The main façade, to the west, consisted of a central terrace enclosed by two large wings, reminiscent of the summerhouse of the Villa Borghese in Rome, and giving the new palace an Italian, baroque air, which the avant-corps with statues mounted on columns, only served to emphasize.

The first floor on either side of the terrace was entirely occupied by the apartments of the King and Queen, each of which contained six main rooms. These became known as the State Apartments to distinguish them from the Private Apartments in the old palace, with which they communicated. No effort was spared in their decoration, which included the rarest materials: polychrome marble, bronze, gilded wood, hangings of embroidered velvet or brocade. Charles Le Brun coordinated the decoration: he supervised the painters and the sculptors, giving them guidelines to follow for a ceiling plan or a statue, right down to the design for a carpet or lock. His creative genius lent itself to innumerable variations in the decoration while maintaining a homogenous character throughout and creating a new style.

The dominant motif in the decoration of the State Apartments was the myth of Apollo. Indeed, Louis XIV had chosen the sun as his emblem from early adolescence, and explained his choice in his memoirs as follows: "The emblem I have always had and which you see in so many places, was chosen to represent the duties of a Prince and to incite me constantly to fulfill them. The sun, in the art of heraldry, is the most noble body of all, which by its unique quality, the radiance which surrounds it, the light it transmits to the stars, which it attracts as to a kind of court, by the fair and harmonious distribution of this same light to all the climes of the planet, by the good it brings to all places, ceaselessly producing life, joy and activity, by its perpetual movement, though it always appears still, by the constant and invariable course it keeps and from which it never deters, the sun is assuredly the most lively and beautiful of images for a Monarch."

Better than any explanation, these wonderful lines reveal how Louis XIV saw his duties and responsabilities, and clarify the symbolism of Versailles, the meaning behind the Sun Palace, which was to be the shining example of Royal Munificence and Justice, of Sovereign Order, and the harmony of Good Government.

The decoration of the State Apartments was therefore inspired by the gods and goddesses who gave their names to the different planets, and, just as these gravitate around the sun, so the Diana, Mars, Mercury, Jupiter, Saturn and Venus Salons enclosed the Apollo Chamber in the King's Apartments, this being his state bedroom before becoming the Throne Room. The ceilings, decorated with paintings and stucco by students of Le Brun, were reproductions of the works of Pietro da Cortona for the Apartment of the Planets in the Pitti Palace in Florence a few years earlier. The divinity occupies the centre while his attributes or emblems evoke the activities of which he is patron: hunting, navigation, war, trade, the arts and sciences. The ceiling paintings refer to great events of the King's reign, barely concealed under a veil of classical allusions. Sumptuous, finely engraved silver furniture adorned the rooms of the King's Apartments, which also housed his collection of antique busts and paintings from the Venetian and Bolognese schools, of which he was so fond, and which today are the

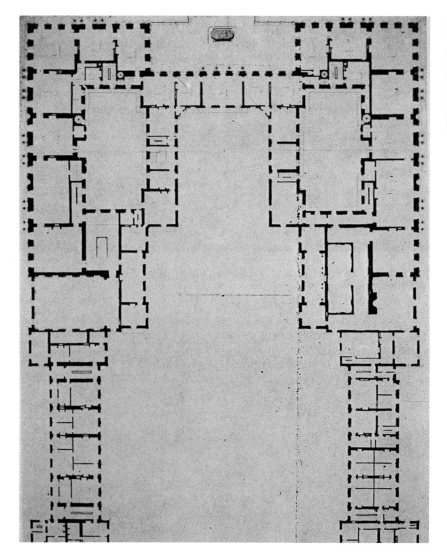

Plan of the first floor of the palace in 1674 – Le Vau's new constructions envelop the original palace on three sides, and the Old Palace itself is linked to the outhouses built in 1662. The King's and Queen's State Apartments extend north and south into the New Palace, on either side of a terrace onto which give their private apartments, located in the Old Palace.

glory of the Louvre Museum. On the ground floor the King installed a bath suite, in keeping with his taste for all that was refined in comfort and luxury.

To provide access to the State Apartments, two new symmetrical staircases were built on either side of the Royal Courtyard. The Queen's, to the south, still stands today, but the Grand Staircase to the north was unfortunately destroyed by Louis XV. This was the most monumental staircase of the palace, and was used during the procession of ambassadors on their way to the Royal Audience. Le Brun had built it using vast quantities of polychrome marble, gilded bronze and trompe l'œil paintings, making the Ambassadors' Staircase a veritable exploit in baroque splendour.

The Grand Staircase, or Ambassadors'
Staircase (model) – This majestic flight of
stairs led to the King's State Apartment.
The floor and walls were covered in
polychrome marble, and the decoration,
with paintings of allegorical figures, false
architectural perspectives, and trompe-
l'œil tapestries, were by Le Brun. The
niche at the stairhead, under a bust of
Louis XIV, contained an antique statue.

THE EXTENSION TO THE PALACE

Meanwhile, the King did not demolish the old palace, rather he embellished it, adding gilded wrought-iron balconies, columns of Rance marble, antique busts set on consoles, and allegorical statues, nonchalantly perched on the ledges of the roof balustrades. Marble slabs were laid in the courtyard, the arcades removed and the ditch these had occupied was filled in. Louis XIII's palace was connected to the outbuildings in 1662 and these were made to blend in with the other buildings by the addition of statues mounted on pillars. A gilded railing linked them up to form another main courtyard called the Cour Royale, or Royal Courtyard.

A little further to the east, two long wings were added to house the Ministers. These enclosed a new forecourt, larger than the old one, and did away with the circular esplanade and the two obelisks. Another gilded railing separated this forecourt from the Place d'Armes, or Parade Ground. It bore the King's monogram on the pediment and a group of statues on either side symbolized the King's victories over the Empire and Spain. The stables were built between the three avenues leading to the palace: the Grande Ecurie or Greater Stables, for the riding horses, and the Petite Ecurie or Lesser Stables for the draught horses and carriages, thus completing the layout. At the same time the vast outhouse was built to the south, below the forecourt, to contain the kitchens, pantries and servants' quarters.

This construction work was completed after the signing of the Treaty of Nijmegen, which represented a triumph for the King over his enemies and confirmed France's pre-eminence in Europe. However, the palace was still far from attaining its definitive form, and the ten years of peace which followed provided the opportunity for another spate of building. It was during this time that the two long wings were added to the north and south ends of the new palace, set back a little way, thereby adding some 600 meters of façade to the garden side. The three wings housed the royal family, princes of the blood, and courtiers. Thus the new palace became the central part of a whole palatial

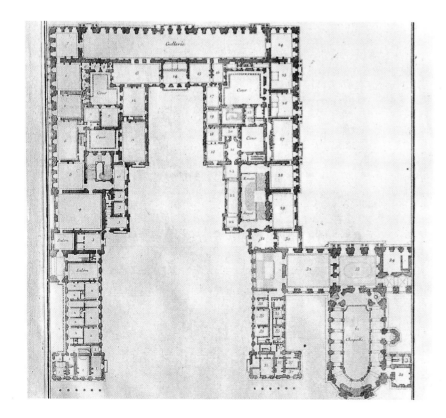

Plan of the first floor of the palace in 1714 – The Gallery of Mirrors has replaced the terrace and the last rooms of the State Apartments. The King's apartment occupies the whole first floor of the Old Palace and the inner courtyards are divided up by the transverse buildings. Note the Grand or Ambassadors' Staircase to the right of the Royal Courtyard.

The Marble Courtyard – The buildings surrounding it date back to Louis XIII, but they were altered and decorated by Louis XIV between 1662 and 1679. He added marble columns, balconies, statues, busts and lead roof decorations which were formerly gilded. The first floor was entirely taken over by the King's apartment.

The clock in the Marble Courtyard (1679) – The statue of Hercules is by Girardon, that of Mars by Gaspard Marsy.

complex, and was itself considerably altered. The terrace on the first floor was removed, along with four of the rooms around it. In their place, Jules Hardouin-Mansart, who succeeded Le Vau as First Architect, built a majestic gallery between two reception rooms. In order to improve the lighting, he enlarged the rectangular windows by arching them. This subtle alteration to Le Vau's architecture is almost imperceptible, even to the expert.

Le Brun was charged with the decoration of this grand gallery, which later became known as the Galerie des Glaces, or Gallery of Mirrors, and he transformed it into one vast epic poem to the King's glory. This time he abandoned mythology and ancient history, and filled the vaulted ceilings with the most glorious events of the first eighteen years of Louis XIV's reign: military and diplomatic victories, civil and economic reforms, the reorganisation of the kingdom, great works, deeds of charity, etc. These paintings were surrounded by gilded stucco, false perspectives, flying figures, painted hangings and trompe l'œil, making the ceiling, and indeed the whole gallery, one of the most striking examples of baroque court art. The seventeen windows in the gallery were matched by the same number of arches, fitted with unusually large mirrors for the time, in gilded bronze frames. Windows and arches were separated by marble pilasters and bronze trophies, as finely engraved as by a master silversmith. Antique statues, busts and porphyry vases, silver furniture, white damask curtains threaded with gold and bearing the King's monogram, all combined to give the Gallery of Mirrors and the two reception rooms on either side of it what the Marquise de Sévigné was to call "a kind of royal beauty, unique in the world".

However, this gallery, which was the culminating point of the suite of rooms which made up the State Apartments, turned the latter into a veritable thoroughfare, and made it quite uninhabitable. Since Queen Marie-Thérèse had died in 1683, before the completion of the gallery, and Louis XIV had secretly married the Marquise de Maintenon, who could not aspire to her predecessor's place at court, the King annexed the former Queen's apartment in the old palace to his own, and made a vast, elegant and extremely comfortable suite for himself there, into which he moved in November 1684. This brought an end to the perfect symmetry which had hitherto characterised the King's and Queen's apartments. This might be interpreted as meaning that his move back to the palace was a temporary one, due to his widowhood and morganatic marriage, but at the time Louis XIV was only forty-six years old and was to live for another thirty-one years. The rebuilding of the old palace was therefore postponed once again, and for quite some time.

A few years later, the King pushed back the southern wall of the old palace towards the centre of the inner courtyard, in order to make space for the guardroom and the vast anterooms he needed. A few years later the same courtyard was divided into two by a building intended to contain the "night apartments" of the King's grandson, the Duc de Bourgogne. The northern courtyard suffered the same fate when a new staircase, the "Shell Study", and the Oval Room were built to facilitate communications with the King's apartments. The result is a series of tiny courtyards which so astonish the visitor today, and which justify the severity of Saint-Simon's criticism concerning the "view of privies and the most somber, enclosed and malodorous things". These

The main part of the palace as seen from the lake – This is how Le Vau's "envelope" appeared after Hardouin-Mansart's transformations. The main terrace and the rooms on either side of it were removed to make way for the Gallery of Mirrors, but a slight difference in the levelling of the façade shows where they once stood.

makeshift arrangements were for the King's convenience and were intended to disappear after him. However, they have survived to this day, but it is a fact that all the great building projects which followed, those of Louis XV like those of Louis XVI, were more or less based on those of Louis XIV, and always aimed at restoring the once perfect symmetry of the King's and Queen's apartments.

The gardens were not neglected during these transformations: vast terracing work laid down the plateau on which the palace grew. A new Orangery was built, far larger than the previous one, the Grand Canal and the Swiss Lake were completed, shrubs were planted under the trees, and a complete network of reservoirs and pipes fed the innumerable fountains.

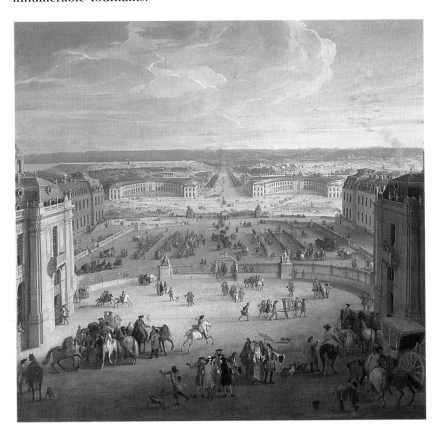

View of the Greater and Lesser Stables as seen from the palace, by Jean-Baptiste Martin, circa 1690 – The Royal Courtyard is in the foreground, separated from the forecourt by gilded railings. Beyond it may be seen the Parade Ground and the Avenue de Paris lying between the two stables.

The central building of the palace as seen from the southern parterre – The Salon of Peace is situated at the corner of the first floor, extending from the Queen's State Apartment on the right. On the ground floor lie the apartments of the Dauphin, son of Louis XV, and the Dauphine.

At the same time a whole town was growing up around the palace, to the design of the King's architect. Stately dwellings were set up to house the servants and staff of the courtiers living in the palace. Further on, the houses of the bourgeoisie, of the craftsmen and tradesmen had sprung up along the streets and squares of the Notre-Dame quarter and the former Parc-aux-Cerfs. This harmonious town, with its numerous parks, was vital to the life of the palace, to which it catered exclusively, and which it framed in one of the most grandiose urban projects ever carried out.

Before the works were even completed, Louis XIV suddenly revealed the reason behind this ambitious enterprise, a project which had taken shape over a number of years: on May 6th, 1682, he ceremoniously

The Palace of Versailles seen from the Orangery – This painting shows how the Orangery parterre looked in the 17th century: note the statues by Borée representing THE KIDNAPPING OF ORYTHIA, today in the Louvre Museum. The Orangery and the Hundred Steps on either side serve to butress the thrust of the ground which was raised to create the southern parterre and provide a magnificent base for the façades of the palace.

moved into Versailles, which he had decided to make his main residence by transferring the court and seat of government there.

The Palace of Versailles seen from the courtyards in 1722, by Pierre-Denis Martin – The gilded railing which frames the group of statues symbolising the Kings's victories over Spain and the Empire, separates the Parade Ground from the forecourt, on either side of which lie the Ministers' Wings. The outhouses are on the left. Another railing, on either side of which stand the statues of Peace and Abundance, separates the forecourt from the Royal Courtyard, to the right of which stands the Chapel. The Marble Courtyard is in the background.

The Orangery – It is composed of three galleries, the main one being 155 meters long, 13 meters wide, and 13.25 meters high. The two secondary galleries, perpendicular to this one, and linked to it by circular avant-corps, are 114.45 meters long. These three stone vessels, with their perfect proportions and fine stonework, shelter the orange trees, pomegranates, and palm trees during the winter months. In the summer these trees, many of which date back as far as Louis XIV, grace the parterres. ▶

Aerial view of the palace, courtyard side. Only an aerial view enables one to understand Le Nôtre's ingenious creation: the three avenues of Saint-Cloud, Paris and Sceaux, which separate the Greater and Lesser Stables, converge on the Parade Ground. Beyond it, the eye travels across the forecourt, enclosed by the Ministers' Wing, to the Royal Courtyard and the Marble Courtyard, which form the centre of the composition.

Aerial view of the palace, garden side. The town, palace and gardens are laid out around the intersection of two axes at which is situated the central avant-corps of the main façade. Behind this avant-corps, lie the lakes, and beyond them, the perrons and ramps which lead to Leto's Parterre. To the right, the southern parterre overlooks that of the Orangery, while to the left, the Northern parterre slopes gently down towards the Water Alley and Neptune's Basin.

THE FIRST KNIGHTS OF SAINT-LOUIS NOMINA-
TED BY LOUIS XIV ON MAY 10th, 1693 – The
artist, François Marot, situated the scene
in the King's State Bedroom after it was
decorated in 1701.

LOUIS XIV AT FONTAINEBLEAU, RECEIVING
THE ELECTOR PRINCE OF SAXONY, ON SEP-
TEMBER 27, 1714 – The Dowager Duchess
d'Orléans is presenting the young prince
to the King, behind whom may be seen the
Duchess de Berry and the Duke and
Duchess d'Orléans. The artist, Louis de
Silvestre, situated the scene in a room
which resembles the King's bedroom in
Versailles far more than the one in
Fontainebleau.

THE CAPITAL OF THE KINGDOM

Henceforth, the affairs of France were governed from Versailles.
Louis XIV's successors respected his wishes and with the interruption
of a brief regency, Versailles was the true political and administrative
capital of the kingdom for a century.

This surprising decision to move the capital, a precursor to such future
projects as Washington and Brasilia, was partly explained by the King's
love of the countryside and of hunting, and the lack of interest he had
in the completion of the Louvre palace, and partly by his wish to create
a palace which reflected the image of his reign. However, it also
reflected the King's desire to protect both the monarch and the
government from subversive activity. He had not forgotten the
humiliation of the Fronde, and remembered from his childhood the
revolt of the bourgeoisie against the Royal Prerogative, when even a
First Prince of the royal blood had allied himself to the "enemies of
the kingdom", thus shaking the very foundations of the monarchy. Versailles' relative distance from Paris meant that he was
protected from day-to-day contact with the Parisian populace and its
dangerous changes of mood. Moreover, the vast and extremely
hierarchical court was an attraction for the nobles and enabled them
to forget past conspiracies in the splendid festivities, and their desire
to please the sovereign. By requiring the nobles to live at court, in
a gilded cage of idleness and semi-domesticity, the King withdrew their
independence, and all desire to revolt with it. In this, as in so many
other things, the King was pursuing the policies of Louis XIII and
Richelieu. Versailles, therefore, became a real instrument of government and the vivid symbol of a whole political system.

The King's decision may be better understood when placed in the
context of the royal policy of administrative centralisation and economic
reform. When Louis XIV took the reins of state in 1661, after
Mazarin's death, it was with the firm intention of ruling himself. Indeed, since he presided the State Council daily and consulted with each
of the ministers in turn, it was necessary for them to live and work
nearby, and government offices had to be installed near the royal
residence.

But the King had no desire to withdraw in splendid isolation: the palace
was open to all, and even the humblest citizen could stroll through the
State Apartments and the gardens, be present at the Royal Supper, or
hand a petition to the King as he made his way to the chapel. General
curiosity, fanned by astute reporting, brought crowds of visitors to the
palace, foreign and French alike, the former under the flattering illusion
that they were attending the most glittering court in Europe, and
everyone left dazzled by the beauty and splendour of the décor which
they were so generously permitted to admire.

Versailles' role in the economic policy of Louis XIV and his minister,
Colbert, was far from negligible. Up to this time, luxury materials such
as marble, velvet, brocade and lace had mostly been imported from
Europe, and Italy in particular. In his desire to stop these costly
imports, so detrimental to the finances of the kingdom, Louis XIV set
up a resolutely protectionist policy. He reopened the marble quarries
in the Pyrenees, which had been abandoned since the fall of the Roman
Empire, and these supplied all the palace marble. He reorganized the
old royal factories and set up new ones, attracting the best craftsmen
in France and Europe with his high wages and good conditions. The
Gallery of Mirrors is, therefore, not only evidence of great magnificence
at a time when mirrors were extremely rare and costly, but proof that
Saint-Gobain had usurped Venice, so that soon Primi Visconti could
write: "The best the world has to offer is now made in France." Versailles
became a sort of permanent exhibition of French arts and crafts, and
it was due to this that within the space of a few years, France was leading

Europe in the manufacture and exportation of luxury items. The new royal residence became the admired and envied model which all the sovereigns of Europe attempted to emulate. Thus the development of French art and the prosperity which the country was to know during the 18th century were in some measure due to the creation of Versailles.

As we have seen, the two long wars which cast a shadow over the latter part of his reign and exhausted the country's resources prevented Louis XIV from completing his project. He who so loved music and dancing, had to abandon the building of the Salle de Ballet which no royal residence could do without. But he did not want to die before he had built the chapel which the palace still lacked. Up to now, he had had to content himself with a number of temporary chapels which were moved around according to the work in progress, and none of which were in any case worthy of the Very Christian King.

The chapel, as it stands today, was begun in 1699 from plans by Mansart, and was completed after the latter's death by his brother-in-law, Robert de Cotte. It stands in front of the north wing, where Thetis' Grotto had been, and its high roof, leading up to a slender bell-tower, proudly dominates the horizontal line of the palace. With its vast dimensions, elegant proportions, and the richness of the interior, the chapel is undoubtedly one of the masterpieces of religious architecture of all time.

LOUIS XIV RECEIVES THE DODGE OF GENOA IN THE GALLERY OF MIRRORS AT VERSAILLES, ON MAY 15th, 1685 – The artist, Claude-Guy Hallé, has depicted the King standing in front of his silver throne, which is placed on a dais at the far end of the Gallery, in front of the arcade of the Salon of Peace. Next to the King stand his son, the Dauphin, his brother, the Duke d'Orléans, and the princes of the blood. Some of the most exquisite pieces of silver furniture surround the throne and provide a clear picture of the magnificence of Versailles at the end of the 17th century.

LOUIS XIV AT THE SWEARING-IN OF THE MARQUIS DE DANGEAU AS GRAND MASTER OF THE ORDERS OF OUR LADY OF MOUNT CARMEL AND ST. LAZARE, ON DECEMBER 18th, 1695 – This painting by Antoine Pezey faithfully depicts the third Chapel of the palace, which was replaced by a reception room in 1710 and later became the Hercules Salon.

18th CENTURY ALTERATIONS

The death of Louis XIV on September 1st, 1715, was followed by a seven-year lull in Versailles, for young Louis XV lived in Paris throughout the Regency. However, as soon as he was proclaimed of age in 1722, he decided to remove the court back to Versailles, where it remained until the Revolution. Louis XV's reign was one of intense artistic activity for the palace, despite a few irreparable losses such as the Bath Suite and the Ambassadors' Staircase. This was counterbalanced by some beautiful creations, not the least of which were the Hercules Salon and the theatre, built at the beginning and end of his reign respectively.

The building of the new chapel had left a vast empty space where the former one had stood, and Louis XIV had intended to use it to install a State Reception Room on the first floor, which would connect the main building with the north wing. However, he died before this was completed, and Louis XV continued the work in 1729, respecting his grandfather's wishes. The marble and gilded bronze decoration blended in with that of the State Apartments into which it led. The ceiling was, however, a new feature for Versailles, in that it was not divided up into sections in the way of those painted by Le Brun, and the result was a feeling of lightness and freshness which recall to mind the fact that the artist, François Le Moyne was, after all, Boucher's master. This whole decoration was designed to fit in with the vast work by Paolo Veronese, MEAL IN THE HOUSE OF SIMON THE PHARISEE, which occupies a whole wall of the room. This painting was given to Louis XIV in 1664 by the Republic of Venice and found a worthy setting in the Hercules Salon.

But, as we have said, Louis XIV did not have time to build the theatre, although he had set aside space for it at the far end of the north wing. Louis XV delayed the work for a long time, and during most of his reign the palace had only a small theatre room in the Court of the Princes, although the King organised private shows in his own apartments, for the benefit of the privileged few. When a large-scale ballet or opera was put on, as on the occasion of a royal wedding for example, a temporary theatre was erected in the ring of the Greater Stables. These temporary arrangements were not worthy of a palace such as Versailles, and Louis XV instructed his First Architect, Ange-Jacques Gabriel, to draw up plans for a definitive theatre, taking into account the prospect of future weddings of the King's grandchildren. Gabriel had had occasion to study the most famous theatres in Europe and observe their good and bad features; he therefore sought to surpass them all. Admirably seconded by the stage designer Arnoult, he built a theatre in two years which was a source of admiration for all his contemporaries and remains unequalled today.

The Royal Theatre was inaugurated on May 16th, 1770, the day of the wedding of the Dauphin, future Louis XVI, and the Archduchess Marie-Antoinette.

LOUIS XV, King of France and Navarra (1710-1774) by Carle Van Loo in 1751.

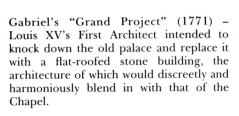

Gabriel's "Grand Project" (1771) – Louis XV's First Architect intended to knock down the old palace and replace it with a flat-roofed stone building, the architecture of which would discreetly and harmoniously blend in with that of the Chapel.

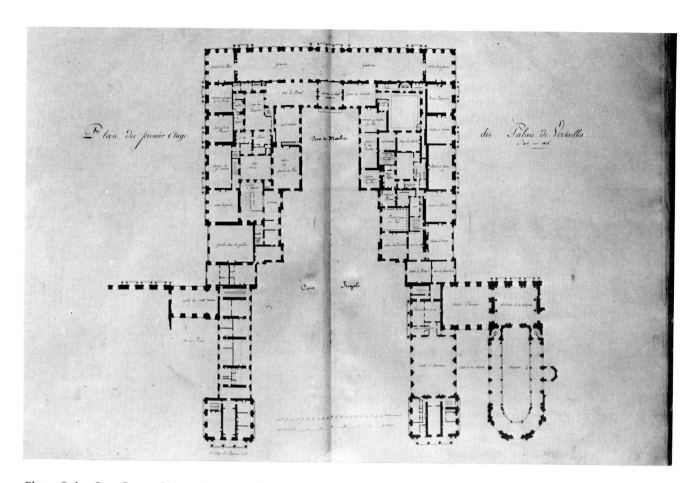

Plan of the first floor of the palace on the eve of the Revolution – The Ambassadors' Staircase was removed to make way for the "new rooms" which enlarged the King's Apartment. Part of the Grand Project was realized: to the right of the Royal Courtyard, the so-called "Government Wing" was partly rebuilt and the future location of the new "Grand Staircase" can be seen.

However, Louis XV was unable to complete one of his great-grandfather's objectives, the "Grand Project" which consisted of rebuilding the façades on the courtyard side in order to harmonize them with the garden side. He finally decided to do this towards the end of his reign, and Louis XVI in turn, was unable to complete the work, which had scarcely begun. Only one stone wing, which disfigures the right side of the Royal Courtyard, bears witness to Gabriel's project. So both Louis XV and Louis XVI lived in Louis XIV's apartments overlooking the Marble Courtyard, while the two Queens Marie Lesczynska and Marie-Antoinette had to make do with a smaller suite than that enjoyed previously by Marie-Thérèse. However, each of them in turn transformed the apartments to make them more comfortable and up-to-date, and produced some gems of 18th-century French decorative art as a result. The Dauphin, the Dauphine and the Mesdames, daughters of the King, who lived on the ground floor of the main palace building, also redecorated their apartments and filled them with beautiful furniture and rare objects. Louis XVI and Marie-Antoinette longed to modernize the solemn palace, and plans were drawn up which would have further accentuated its gigantic aspect, but these were never realized because of the Revolution.

LOUIS XVI, King of France and Navarra (1754-1793) by Duplessis in 1775.

TRIANON

Work on this building, which was started in 1772, was only completed at the beginning of the 19th century. It is in fact half of a wing designed by Gabriel for his "Grand Project" and never completed. It houses the new Grand Staircase.

From the start, this small estate, located inside the Little Park and surrounded by walls, seems to have been set aside for the entertainment of the Royal Family. Indeed, its building coincided with the first large-scale additions to Versailles, as if the King wished to preserve somewhere the intimate character of the palace of his youth.

The name Trianon belonged to a hamlet, the existance of which dates back to the Middle Ages. Louis XIV bought the original houses in 1663 in order to enlarge his domain, and these were torn down two years later and their inhabitants housed elsewhere. In 1667 the village church was also pulled down.

It was on this site that Le Vau built, in 1670, "a porcelain house for taking refreshments", as Saint-Simon described it. For the walls were of blue and white porcelain tiles, which made it resemble a kind of pagoda. Indeed, at this time missionaries returning from the East were firing the imagination of the French with their tales of China, and it had become fashionable to collect exquisite Chinese porcelain. The interior decoration and the furniture of the Trianon were also predominantly blue and white, and similar tiles covered the walls of the four outhouses, in which meat was hung and food and jams were prepared.

According to the architect Felibien, "this palace seemed at first to be magic, for although it was only begun at the end of winter, it was completed by the spring, as if it had risen from the earth along with the garden flowers all around it." In fact the main charm of Trianon were the gardens, for the flower beds were changed every day, sometimes twice a day, and with its arbours of jasmine, and orange trees planted in open soil, it was a veritable "kingdom of Flora".

However, this "Porcelain Trianon" "was not destined to last for long." Its upkeep was costly, as the tiles had to be replaced every year because of frost damage. Moreover, the King's taste had changed and

The "Porcelain Trianon", seen from the approach (engraving by Pérelle) – The main courtyard which lies in front of the central pavillion is framed by four secondary pavillions, where the soups, entrées, roasts, second courses and jams were prepared.

he no longer enjoyed the whimsical constructions of his youth. Now that he had settled definitively in Versailles, he wanted a small palace where he could rest, away from the cares of state and the chores of ceremony.

In 1687 Mansart replaced the "Porcelain Trianon" with the "Marble Trianon", or, as Saint-Simon put it, "a little palace of marble and porphyry, with delightful gardens." This building was larger than the former one, but the King stayed there with a reduced suite, for only his direct family was allowed, and service was kept to a minimum. Even princes of the blood had to ask permission if they wanted to dine there. Occasionaly, Louis XIV would permit his courtiers to visit the Trianon. Saint-Simon wrote that "nothing was so marvellous as those evenings in the Trianon. The flower beds were changed daily, and I have seen the King and the whole court being forced to leave the gardens because the lingering fragrance of the tuberoses was so overwhelming that none could remain, and this despite the fact that the garden was large, terraced, and gave onto a bend in the canal". Louis XV showed little interest in the Trianon at first, but from 1750 he began to develop a liking for it and started to go there frequently. He began by building a New Menagerie, where domestic animals were reared and selected. Soon after, he planted a Botanical Garden, in which exotic plants such as pineapple, coffee, geranium and strawberry were cultivated, and wheat rot was studied.

To enable the King to pursue his scientific experiments, and collate and classify his herbarium at his leisure, Gabriel built a charming pavillion in the middle of a French-style garden. A few years later he also built a little palace at the bottom of the garden, so that the King could stay for short periods in the place he liked so much. This became known as the Petit Trianon, and the architect deployed his skills to the utmost.

MARIE-ANTOINETTE, Queen of France and Navarra (1755-1793) by Louise-Elizabeth Vigée-Lebrun in 1784.

The "Porcelain Trianon" seen from the garden side (engraving by Pérelle) – The garden is divided into two plots: the lower one, in the foreground, is graced with orange trees and arbours of jasmin.

The Queen's House in the Hamlet – This house is in fact made up of two buildings linked by a wooden gallery: the "billiards house" on the left and the Queen's house itself on the right. The latter consists of a dining room, a large drawing room and three other rooms. The gallery and outside staircase are decorated with china flower pots bearing Marie-Antoinette's monogram.

The Battle Gallery – This gallery, 120 meters long and 13 meters wide, was installed by Louis-Philippe in the place of four apartments which formerly belonged to princes of the blood. The thirty-five paintings hanging here all represent great victories in French history from Tolbiac (496) to Wagram (1809).

No sooner did Louis XVI come to the throne, than he offered the Little Trianon to Marie-Antoinette. In the fashion of the time, she wanted "picturesque" English-style gardens, with lawns, a winding river, a lake and garden houses. She removed Louis XV's botanical garden and sent the plants to the Jardin du Roi, or King's Garden, in Paris. Later on, Mique built her a delightful theatre and a little hamlet complete with model farm. That was to be the last royal construction in Trianon, a place which always reflected the human, informal side of Versailles.

THE NATIONAL MUSEUM

On the eve of the Revolution, Versailles was the most sumptuous royal residence with the most glittering court imaginable, greatly admired by all of Europe. The works of art collected by the various Kings over the century also made it a unique museum. But on October 6th, 1789, popular pressure obliged Louis XVI to return to Paris. Less than three years later the monarchy was abolished, the palace was never inhabited again, and the dispersal of its treasures had begun.

As early as September 1792, a "Provisional Arts Commission" was set up to distribute the former royal collections. Paintings, antiques and gems were sent to the "Museum", the present Louvre, while books and medals were sent to the National Library. Clocks and scientific instruments went to the Conservatoire National des Arts et Métiers (the National Conservatory of Arts and Crafts). With a few rare exceptions, all the royal furniture was auctioned off over a period of three years. The palace was now empty, but it was decided that "it should be preserved and kept up by the Republic for the people's pleasure, and for the use of organisations in the fields of agriculture and the arts." In 1797 a natural history museum, a library, and an academy of music were set up in the former palace, as well as a special museum of the French school of art, which exhibited some three hundred and fifty paintings, including twenty-three Poussins, and the two hundred and fifty statues from the palace gardens. But this museum did not last for long: a few years later all the paintings were sent off to the Louvre. When Napoleon proclaimed the Empire, Versailles became a Crown Residence again, and Napoleon began to restore it methodically, as he did with all the royal palaces which had been spared during the Revolution. He had even decided to spend three months a year there during the summer, but his abdication in April 1814 prevented him from ever carrying out this plan. Similarly, the Restoration was too short to allow Louis XVIII or Charles X the time to settle, as they had wished, in the palace in which they were born.

In 1830, the palace was still practically intact, but its fate was uncertain. Scorned by public opinion as the symbol of absolute monarchy, it was threatened, at worst with demolition, and at best with being turned into a military hospital, or school of agriculture. In order to save it from possible destruction, or being put to degrading use, the new King, Louis-Philippe, persuaded Parliament to attribute it to him, on condition that he convert it into a history museum devoted "to the glory of France", at his own expense. He hoped, that by exalting the highlights of French history, he might reunite the French people, then split into four factions: the Legitimists, faithful to the deposed king, Charles X; the Orléanists, who favoured Louis-Philippe; the Republicans, attached to the great ideals of the Revolution; and the Bonapartists, who looked back with nostalgia to the heyday of Napoleon.

Between 1833 and 1837, the former palace was transformed into an enormous building site while work was in progress to convert it into a museum. The architect, Frédéric Nepveu, supervised the work, and the King made weekly inspections to check on progress and give

LOUIS-PHILIPPE THE FIRST, King of the French (1773-1850) by Franz Winterhalter in 1839.

orders. In four years he visited the place no less than 398 times, but unfortunately he thought nothing of destroying most of the apartments of the princes and courtiers in order to create the vast exhibition halls he needed. Thus on the ground floor of the main building, were lost the apartments of the Dauphin, the Dauphine and the Mesdames, the daughters of Louis XV, which had been among the richest and most elegant in the palace. However, in doing this, he was perfectly attuned to the taste of his time. In a book entitled *Descriptive Portrait of the Palace of Versailles*, the author Vaysse de Villiers wrote the following: "The public is never shown the rooms on the ground floor. All the rooms, with the exception of one containing some carved and gilded decoration, are little more than plaster and panelling, with a few paintings over the doors and some mirrors... I can assure readers that what they are not shown does not merit their attention and is not worth regretting."

In other words, Louis-Philippe sacrificed the many to spare the few, but he did manage to save the chapel, the theatre, the Gallery of Mirrors, and most of the interior decoration in the royal apartments. The new museum was inaugurated on June 10th, 1837, on the occasion of the wedding of the Prince Royal, heir to the throne. Those who sympathize with the Citizen King would agree that he "transformed a palace devoted to the apotheosis of one man into a palace dedicated to the glory of a nation."

Indeed, Louis-Philippe wanted the former palace of Louis XIV to honour the great men and events of French history. With this in mind, he collected all the portraits he could find in the various royal collections, as well as paintings depicting historical events. Thus he saved from oblivion, if not destruction, a number of works of remarkable documentary value and artistic merit. Thanks to him, Versailles houses paintings by Philippe de Champaigne, Le Brun, Mignard, Rigaud, Largillière, Van der Meulen, Parrocel, Van Loo, Nattier, Tocqué, Natoire, Drouais, Hubert Robert, Vigée Le Brun, Labille-Guiard, David, Gros, Gérard, Delacroix, Horace Vernet and Winterhalter, as well as sculptures by Girardon, Coysevox, Coustou, Le Moyne, Pajou, Caffiéri and Houdon.

However, for a long time these works were hung side by side with mediocre ones that the King had added to complete collections, which explains why successive curators have weeded out copies and retrospective works. Since then, only original works have been hung, that is to say works by contemporaries of the persons or events depicted. The only exceptions to this rule are the paintings in the Crusader Rooms and the Battle Gallery, which are significant examples of historical themes as treated in the 19th century. These rooms and a few others have retained Louis-Philippe's decoration, and bear witness to a period of transition in the history of museology.

The Citizen King's enterprise was based on a firm belief in the existence of a feeling of national unity, represented by Versailles. In his desire to lay down a framework for the reconciliation of the French people, he did his utmost to enable them to identify with the palace and become united in their common heritage. This lofty ambition came under a great deal of criticism during his lifetime, and particularly after his fall. However, modern historians are more objective, and by emphasizing his aims and pointing out the limitations of his vast enterprise, by analysing its merits as well as its shortcomings, they give him the credit that was so long denied him.

Certainly the National Museum of the Palace of Versailles is no longer the one which Louis-Philippe laid out. However, it has, on the whole, kept its dual character of museum-cum-residence, so dear to the heart of its founder, when he chose to integrate the "History Galleries" to what remained of the original decoration in the former palace.

Since then, and still with this dual perspective in mind, the collections have regularly been added to. Since the Second World War, a policy of systematically restoring the wall decorations and furniture has succeeded in saving much of what escaped the 19th-century alterations, thereby returning some of its former splendour to the most famous of royal residences.

The Grand Staircase – This replaced the Ambassadors' Staircase which was torn down in 1752. Although work began on this staircase in 1772 from plans by Gabriel, it was only completed in 1985! It leads to the Hercules Salon at the entrance of the King's State Apartment.

THE STATE APARTMENTS

The King's State Apartments were set up in 1670 on the first floor of the New Palace facing north, and the name stuck long after the King ceased to live there. At the time it was composed of seven rooms: the reception room, onto which the Grand Staircase gave, the guardroom, the anteroom, the bedroom, and three private rooms, the last of which gave onto the main terrace, beyond which lay the Queen's State Apartments.

Two new rooms were soon added to the east side of this suite of rooms, while the building of the Gallery of Mirrors eliminated the last two rooms on the other side. At the end of Louis XIV's reign a vast reception room was built, which later became the Hercules Salon, and this provided a new access to the State Apartment by connecting it to the Chapel and the north wing. As early as 1684, Louis XIV moved into a new apartment on the first floor of the Old Palace, which was, in fact, none other than his former "private apartment", much enlarged. The State Apartment was therefore reduced to being a mere passageway leading to the Gallery of Mirrors, but on certain days, so-called "apartment days", the King, the royal family and the whole Court would gather there for four hours in the evening, between six and ten o'clock. On this occasion each room was devoted to a particular pursuit, etiquette was relaxed, and the King was a mere host, presiding over the entertainment of his guests.

The State Apartment was also something of a museum, in which Louis XIV exhibited the masterpieces of his collections: statues and antique busts in marble-lined rooms, paintings in other rooms draped with embroidered velvet, brocade or damask.

MEAL IN THE HOUSE OF SIMON THE PHARISEE by Paolo Veronese – This huge painting came from the convent of the Servites in Venice. In 1664 it was given by the Republic of Venice to Louis XIV, who was known for his fondness for Venetian painting, and it was hung here in 1736. The lavish frame was carved by Jacques Verberckt.

A detail from the ceiling – Painted by François Le Moyne between 1733 and 1736, the ceiling depicts the APOTHEOSIS OF HERCULES. The demi-god arrives in his charriot before Jupiter and Juno in Olympus, where they present his future wife Hebe to him. All the gods and goddesses of mythology can be seen here in a variety of beautiful poses.

The fireplace in the Hercules Salon – It is decorated with bronze and above it hangs a painting by Paolo Veronese entitled THE MEETING BETWEEN ELIEZER AND REBECCA.

◄ The Hercules Salon – Begun in 1712 on the site of the third chapel, this magnificent room was only finished in 1736. Its marble pilasters with gilded bronze capitals is reminiscent of those in the Gallery of Mirrors, situated at the opposite end of the suite. Some of Louis XV and Louis XVI's most sparkling entertainments were held here: full-dress balls, dinners, receptions for ambassadors and so on.

Detail of the fireplace – Hercules' face was powerfully sculpted by Antoine Vassé.

The Salon of Abundance – During "Apartment Evenings" this little reception room held the buffet. Three tables were brought in laden with gold and silver pots containing coffee, cocoa, lemonade, iced water, sorbets and a variety of liqueurs.

The Venus Salon – Like the neighbouring Diana Salon, this opened on to the Ambassadors' Staircase and served as a kind of vestibule to the State Apartment. On "Apartment Evenings" refreshments were served here and tables were covered with silver bowls full of preserves, fresh and crystallized fruit.

◀◀ Ceiling of the Salon of Abundance – The artist René-Antoine Houasse depicted ROYAL MUNIFICENCE AND THE PROGRESS OF THE ARTS. The medals which are spilling out of the horn of plenty and the gems on the false cornices, represent the King's collections which were kept in the "Rare Objects Room", to which this salon served as anteroom.

◀ PHILIP V, King of Spain (1683-1746), by Hyacinthe Rigaud in 1701.

Ceiling of the Venus Salon – In the centre Houasse depicted VENUS SUBJUGATING THE GODS AND POWERS TO HER EMPIRE. ▶

43

False architectural perspectives in the Venus Salon, the work ▶
of Jacques Rousseau.

LOUIS XIV by Jean Warin – The statue
◀ represents the King in roman dress.

The ceiling of the Diana Salon–Gabriel Blanchard painted
DIANA PRESIDING OVER HUNTING AND NAVIGATION.

THE SACRIFICE OF IPHIGENIA, by Charles de La Fosse.

LOUIS XIV by Lorenzo Bernini in 1665 – This beautiful piece of workmanship is one of this Roman sculptor's great masterpieces, and the finest portrait of the King in the full bloom of youth.

◄ The Diana Salon – The door to the right of the King's bust opened onto the Ambassadors' Staircase; this room was therefore the second vestibule in the State Apartment, and also served as a billiards room.

QUEEN MARIE LESZCYNSKA, by Carle Van Loo in 1747.

▶The Mars Salon – During "Apartment Evenings" this room was set aside for music. Above the fireplace hangs KING DAVID by Domenico Zampieri, to the left DARIUS' FAMILY AT ALEXANDER'S FEET, by Charles Le Brun, and to the right PILGRIMS FROM EMMAUS by Veronese. At the far end hangs a PORTRAIT OF LOUIS XV by Carle Van Loo.

DARIUS' FAMILY AT THE FEET OF ALEXANDER THE GREAT, by Charles Le Brun.

◀◀The ceiling of the Mars Salon – MARS ON HIS CHARRIOT by Houasse. The arms trophies and the trompe l'œil bas-reliefs evoke French victories and the reorganization of the army.

◀A detail from the ceiling in the Mars Salon – The martial decoration is a reminder that this room was originally the guardroom.

The Mercury Salon – This room was an antechamber before
becoming a state bedroom. On "Apartment Evenings" it
was used by the royal family for games.

LOUIS XV IN CORONATION ROBES, by Hyacinthe Rigaud in 1730.

QUEEN MARIE LESZCYNSKA, by Louis Tocqué in 1740.

Commode made by André-Charles Boulle in 1709 for the bedroom of Louis XIV at Trianon.

Ceiling of the Mercury Salon – MERCURY IN HIS CHARRIOT WITH THE MORNING STAR, THE ARTS AND THE SCIENCES by Jean-Baptiste de Champaigne.

Pedestal figure carved by Babel – This table and the following one belonged to a series of twenty-four made for the Gallery of Mirrors in 1769. Today they are replaced by copies.

The Apollo Salon – This was the King's bedroom before becoming the Throne Room. The silver throne was placed on a dais under a canopy. Today the spot is marked by a tapestry.

Pedestal stand carved
by Toussaint Foliot.

The ceiling of the Apollo Salon – Charles de La Fosse depicted APOLLO IN HIS CHARRIOT, ACCOMPANIED BY THE FIGURE OF FRANCE AND THE PROCESSION OF SEASONS. In the corners may be seen allegorical representations of the Four Continents.

LOUIS XIV IN CORONATION ROBES, by Hyacinthe Rigaud in 1701–This famous portrait always hung over the fireplace in the Apollo Salon.

THE GRAND GALLERY
OR GALLERY OF MIRRORS

This occupied what had been the last two rooms of the King's State Apartment, the main terrace, and the last two rooms of the Queen's State Apartment. The State Reception Rooms of the King and Queen were replaced by the War and Peace Reception Rooms on either side of the Gallery of Mirrors.

This majestic gallery, which was the culminating point of the suite of rooms which made up the State Apartment, was built by Jules Hardouin-Mansart between 1678 and 1686. Charles Le Brun was charged with the decoration, and the ceiling paintings representing the great events of the first eighteen years of Louis XIV's reign, are his own work.

The Gallery of Mirrors was really a kind of anteroom; since it was the only means by which the King and Queen could make their daily visit to the Chapel, crowds of people would gather there in order to admire the brilliant procession, and petitioners would take the opportunity to press their claims on the King.

But the Gallery of Mirrors was also a magnificent setting for the great festivities held at Court: the full-dress or masked balls given on the occasion of a royal wedding, and in particular the receptions held for an Ambassador Extraordinary. On this occasion the silver throne would be placed under a canopy before the arch of the Salon of Peace, on a rostrum covered with a Persian carpet with a gold background. On such occasions the Gallery of Mirrors really took on what the Marquise de Sévigné was to call "a kind of royal beauty, unique in the world".

The cupola of the War Salon, painted by Le Brun – At the centre, France in armour, with Louis XIV on her shield, and in the coving, the Empire, Spain and Holland uniting against France.

Gilded bronze trophy, worked by Ladoireau. ▶

◀ The War Salon – This was formerly the King's Audience Chamber.

PAINTINGS ON THE VAULTED CEILING

*1. THE ALLIANCE OF GERMANY AND SPAIN WITH HOLLAND IN 1672.

2. COMPENSATION FOR THE CORSICAN ATTACK, 1664.

3. HELPING THE PEOPLE DURING FAMINE, 1662.

4. TO THE AID OF HOLLAND AGAINST THE BISHOP OF MUNSTER, 1665.

*5. THE KING TAKES MAËSTRICHT IN THIRTEEN DAYS, 1673.

*6. CROSSING THE RHINE IN THE PRESENCE OF THE ENEMY, 1672.

7. FRANCE'S SUPREMACY RECOGNIZED BY SPAIN, 1662.

8. FURY AT THE BANNING OF DUELS, 1662.

9. DEFEAT OF THE TURKS IN HUNGARY BY THE KING'S TROOPS, 1664.

*10. THE KING FORTIFYING THE LAND AND THE SEAS, 1672.

*11. THE KING GIVING ORDERS FOR THE SIMULTANEOUS ATTACK ON FOUR STRONGHOLDS IN HOLLAND, 1672.

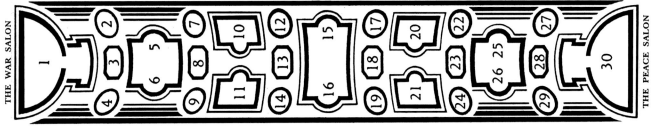

THE WAR SALON

THE PEACE SALON

29. ALLIANCE WITH THE SWISS RENEWED, 1663.
*30. HOLLAND ACCEPTS PEACE AND BREAKS WITH GERMANY AND
SPAIN, 1678.

REPRODUCED ON PAGES 58-59

12. LAW REFORM, 1667.
13. WAR AGAINST SPAIN FOR THE QUEEN'S RIGHTS, 1667.
14. RESUMPTION OF NAVIGATION, 1663.
*15. POMP OF NEIGHBOURING POWERS.
*16. THE KING GOVERNS ON HIS OWN, 1661.
17. PATRONAGE OF THE ARTS, 1663.
18. PEACE CONCLUDED AT AIX-LA-CHAPELLE, 1668.
19. ORDER RETURNED TO FINANCE, 1662.
*20. RESOLUTION TAKEN TO DECLARE WAR ON THE DUTCH, 1671.

*21. FRANCHE-COMTÉ CAPTURED FOR THE SECOND TIME, 1674.
22. AMBASSADORS FROM THE FOUR CORNERS OF THE EARTH.
23. ACQUISITION OF DUNKIRK, 1662.
24. THE HÔTEL ROYAL DES INVALIDES ESTABLISHED, 1674.
*25. SPAIN RETREATING AFTER THE CAPTURE OF GAND.
*26. THE TOWN AND THE CITADEL OF GAND TAKEN IN SIX DAYS, 1678.
27. MEETING OF TWO SEAS, 1667.
28. POLICE AND SECURITY IN PARIS, 1665.

The Gallery of Mirrors, rythmically punctuated by marble pilasters, gilded bronze trophies and niches containing antique statues. Eight busts of Roman Emperors in porphyry and vases complete the decoration. The pedestal figures on which the girandoles stand, are modern copies, the original ones being exhibited in the Apollo Salon.

Urania, the muse of astronomy.

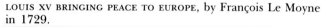

Cupola of the Peace Salon: victorious France bestowing peace on the very nations that had united against her, and which now return joyfully to their previous occupations.

The Salon of Peace, similar in decoration to that of the Salon of War, but with a theme of peace.   During the 18th century this was the Queen's Games Room.   The concerts held here every Sunday by Marie Leszcynska had an important influence on the musical history of France.

LOUIS XV BRINGING PEACE TO EUROPE, by François Le Moyne in 1729.

THE ROYAL CHAPEL

Work on this majestic building, which replaced a succession of provisional chapels, was begun in 1699 after plans by Jules Hardouin-Mansart, and finished in 1710 under Robert de Cotte. In keeping with tradition in palace chapels, it is two storeys high and the gallery, reserved for the Royal Family and the most important persons of the Court, was directly connected with the State Apartments.

Its brightness is enhanced by the white stone used, and heightened by the golds of the high altar and the organ, while the delicate polychrome marble flagstones and ceiling paintings emphasize the noble architectural lines. The paintings themselves represent the three persons of the Holy Trinity, while the pillar sculptures, beautifully carved by the greatest sculptors of the day, delicately convey the parallels between the Old and New Testaments.

The King himself ensured the quality of the accoustics, for the daily mass was always accompanied by music: the triumphant chords of the organ alternating with motet, choir or orchestra.

Throughout the 18th century, the Chapel was the setting for all the religious ceremonies of the Court, from the King's daily mass to royal baptisms and weddings or the swearing-in of the Knights of the Holy Ghost.

◄ The Chapel seen from the Royal Tribune.

The Crucifixion – The statues in the ground floor arcades mark the stages of the Way of the Cross.

Anteroom to the chapel – This huge room, the architecture and decoration of which are similar to those of the chapel next to it, forms the link between the Royal Tribune and the State Apartment. In the niche stands MAGNAMITY, a statue by Jacques Bousseau.

The Cliquot organ at the centre of the choir and musicians' tribune. Above it, THE RESURRECTION OF CHRIST, by Charles de La Fosse.

The Royal Tribune where the King and the royal family generally stood. Above it, THE HOLY SPIRIT DESCENDING ON THE VIRGIN AND THE APOSTLES ON THE EVENING OF PENTECOST, painted by Jean Jouvenet.

◀ The vault of the nave – In the centre Antoine Coypel painted GOD THE FATHER IN ALL HIS GLORY. The Four Evangelists are depicted on the face of the painted medallions, as well as Charlemagne and Saint Louis to whom the chapel was dedicated. Between the high windows the Prophets prefigure the Apostles who may be seen on the ceilings of the side tribunes.

The High Altar – This wonderful piece of craftsmanship was the work of Corneille Van Clève from drawings by Robert de Cotte. He made the nimbus around Jehova's triangle, the three great angels and the bas-relief depicting the Virgin with Christ's body on her lap.

THE KING'S APARTMENT

Louis XIV created this new apartment in 1684 by joining up his former "private apartment" to that of Queen Marie-Thérèse, who had died a few months earlier. The result was a spacious and comfortable apartment which occupied the whole of the first floor of the Old Palace. He had it decorated in the latest style, with finely carved gilded panelling, and the result was a youthful and cheerful appearance which contrasted with the imposing luxury of the State Apartments. Some rooms were even lined with mirrors, reflecting the most precious objects of the royal collections.

If the first rooms were devoted to the King's public life: the "Lever" and "Coucher" ceremonies, meals taken in public, royal audiences and meetings of the council, the inner rooms were given over to the collectioner's pleasure. For it was in these inner rooms, to which only the privileged few were admitted, generally art-lovers like the King, that Louis XIV jealously guarded the masterpieces of his collections. This not only included famous paintings like Leonardo da Vinci's MONA LISA, or Titian's PASTORALE, but also his splendid gold medal collection, and the fabulous crown jewels, marvellous objects of jasper, agate, lapis lazuli and rock crystal, set in gem-encrusted gold, which may be found in the Apollo Gallery of the Louvre today.

Louis XV kept the anterooms and the bedroom in which Louis XIV died, but after 1738 he completely transformed the inner rooms from a kind of museum into a veritable private apartment. The craftsmen Verberckt and Rousseau carved beautiful panelling after drawings by Gabriel, which enhanced the magnificent furniture, created by the most famous cabinet-makers, silks from Lyon, carpets from La Savonnerie and porcelain from Sèvres. Louis XVI later added an elegant library in which he could indulge his love of reading.

◄ The First Anteroom – This room was decorated with a series of paintings by Parrocel representing famous battles of antiquity. It was in this room that Louis XIV dined in the presence of his subjects, every evening at ten o'clock.

◄ The Second Anteroom, known also as the "Salon de l'œil de Bœuf" (Ox-Eye Salon). Here courtiers waited to be admitted to the King's bedroom. The room is decorated with royal portraits and busts of Louis XIV, Louis XV, and Louis XVI. This one of LOUIS XIV is by Coysevox.

BATTLE WITH BODYGUARDS FIGHTING by Jacques Parrocel – This painting always hung above the fireplace in the Guardroom.

BATTLE SCENE by Parrocel.

Detail of the frieze in the Ox-Eye Salon – The room's charm lies in this ring of laughing children carved by Van Clève, Poulletier, Hardy, Poirier, Hurtrelle and Flamen.

LOUIS XIV AND THE ROYAL FAMILY, by Jean Nocret – This curious painting, in which the Olympian gods and goddesses bear the features of the King and members of his family, originally came from the Château de Saint-Cloud.

The King's Bedroom – This beautiful room located at the ▶ centre of the apartment was originally a drawing room which gave on to the Gallery of Mirrors by means of three arcades. In 1701 Louis XIV had it converted into a bedroom for himself and Nicolas Coustou carved the bas-relief representing FRANCE WATCHING OVER THE SLEEPING KING. Louis XIV died here on September 1st, 1715.

THE LAST CAESAR, by Valentin de Boulogne.

SELF-PORTRAIT by Anthony Van Dyck – Louis XIV had this beautiful portrait hanging over one of the doors in his room, a sign of his eclectic tastes.

LOUIS XIV, by Antoine Coysevox.

Bust of Alexander the Great in porphyry, marble and gilded bronze. Louis XV himself had it placed in this room.

Mantelpiece in the Council Room – The extraordinary rococo clock was made for Louis XV in 1754. The Sèvres porcelain vases with the bronze figures of Mars and Minerva by Thomire, were ordered by Louis XVI especially for this mantlepiece, in 1787. ▲

Detail of the crimson and gold brocade which covered the walls of the bed-recess.

Detail of panelling in the Cabinet Doré (Gilded Room), by Degoullons (early part of Louis XV's reign).

The Council Room – Here the King presided over the Council of Ministers and held his audiences.

The new Bedchamber – Louis XV had this room installed for himself in 1738, after which time he used Louis XIV's room for audiences and the "Lever" and "Coucher" ceremonies. It was here that he died on May 10th, 1774.

The brocaded lampas silk which covered the walls of the ▶ bed-recess in the new bedchamber. This was Louis XVI's last "summer furnishing", in place on October 6th, 1789, the day the King was forced to leave the palace.

"Scent fountain" in Chinese porcelain and gilded bronze, ▶▶ delivered to Louis XV by the merchant Hébert, for the King's wardrobe in Versailles.

Detail of the panelling in the Council Chamber, by Antoine Rousseau in 1755.

74

◀ The King's Wardrobe Room – The decoration dates to 1788.   The panelling by the Rousseau brothers depicts emblems of agriculture, commerce, war, shipping, and the arts and sciences.

The Science Panel – The scientific instruments integrated to the arabesques, form the focal point of the decoration.

◀ The Hounds' Room – This room, which opened on the King's private staircase, served as an anteroom for the private drawing room.   The panelling dates from 1684 and comes from Louis XIV's former billiard room.

A painting by Blin de Fontenay above the door in the Hounds' Room.

The Clock Cabinet – This room was created in 1738 and altered in 1760. In the daytime it served as an ante-chamber to the King's private rooms, and in the evening it doubled up as a games room.

Panelling in the Clock Cabinet, carved by Verberckt in 1738 ▶ after drawings by Gabriel. The table base was made by Roumier in 1737 for the King's rooms in Versailles.

▶ The so-called "return from the hunt" Dining Room – Installed in 1750, it was for many years the setting for the King's supper parties after a day's hunting.

◀ The King's Staircase – This constituted the normal access to the King's private rooms. It also led to the Private Apartment on the second floor and on the ground floor it gave out onto the Guards' Room.

One of two corner cupboards from the Drawing Room – The pair was made by Joubert in 1755 to go with the medal cabinet.

◄ The Astronomical Clock – The work of the engineer Passement, the clock-maker Dauthiau and the bronze-founder Caffiéri, this extraordinary instrument was delivered to the palace in 1754 for the Clock Cabinet to which it gave the name. The clock gives the day, month, day of the month, lunar quarter and movement of the planets.

The Medal Cabinet – This fine piece of furniture was made by Gaudreaux in 1738 from a design by the Slodtz brothers, who also designed the bronze decoration. The cabinet housed the King's gold medal collection. The American Independence candelabrum and the two Sèvres porcelain vases were ordered by Louis XVI.

The King's Private Drawing Room – Located at the angle between the Marble Courtyard and the Royal Courtyard, this was formerly Louis XIV's Exhibition Room for Paintings, which Louis XV made into a study. With its beautiful decoration and magnificent furniture, it is one of the most beautiful rooms in the palace.

Detail of the panelling in the King's Drawing Room – The medallions depicting children's games were made by Jacques Verberckt.

The Rear Study – Louis XV would shut himself in this room in order to write to the secret agents whom he sent abroad, or to read their reports. It was therefore the headquarters of his personal diplomacy, the "King's secret".

The Gold Plate Room – From 1753 this was Madame ▶ Adélaïde's private drawing room. Her apartment was next to that of the King, and was taken over by Louis XV in 1769 from his daughter.

THE SULTANA GIVING ORDERS TO THE ODALISQUES – This Sèvres porcelain plaque, along with the one from which it hangs, were ordered by Louis XVI for his private drawing room.

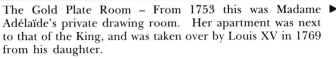

Detail of the panelling in the Gold Plate Room, carved by ▶ Verberckt in 1753.

Cabinet by Benneman – This rare piece of furniture made ▶▶ for Louis XVI is made from mahogany, ebony, and gilded bronze, with porcelain inserts decorated with bird feather and butterfly wing motifs.

The Bathroom – Installed in 1773 for Louis XV, this was to be the last one made for him. Louis XVI transformed it into the Privy-Purse Room.

Panelling in the bathroom, the work of the Rousseau brothers, depicting aquatic pleasures.

The Library – This was installed by Gabriel in 1775 for Louis XVI, in what was Madame Adélaïde's former bedroom, which Louis XV had transformed into a games room. The round table is by Riesener.

The fireplace in the library – The sculptures are by Boizot and the bronze figures by Gouthière. The mantelpiece was placed here for Louis XVI and originally came from one of Madame Du Barry's former drawing rooms in the Palace of Fontainebleau.

Detail of the panelling, which depicts different styles of poetry, and was made by Antoine Rousseau from drawings by Gabriel.

The "new" Dining Room – This room was made in 1769 by joining up Madame Adélaïde's anteroom and audience chamber, and replaced the so-called "after the hunt" dining room – The paintings above the doors are by Collin de Vermont and represent Ovid's Metamorphoses.

The Games Room – This stood in the place of Louis XIV's former "Rare Objects Room" and was where Louis XVI and his hunting companions would round off their evening with a game.

RALLYING AT THE KING'S WELL – This is one of nine Sèvres porcelain plaques made for Louis XVI after J.B. Oudry's THE HUNTS OF LOUIS XV.

One of four corner-cupboards from the Games Room made by Riesener in 1785.

One of the chairs from the Games Room – Boulard produced thirty such chairs, covered with crimson and gold brocade.

SIEGE OF FRIBOURG FROM SEPTEMBER 30 TO NOVEMBER 17TH, 1744, by Van Blarenberghe.

THE KING'S PRIVATE APARTMENT

Above his official apartment, Louis XV installed his private apartment over several floors, to which he would readily flee, alone or with a few chosen friends, in order to escape the servitude of etiquette. Here he had libraries, drawing rooms, winter and summer dining rooms where he would invite his companions to dinner after a day's hunting, kitchens, terraces, and aviaries. This was his secret territory, little known to the public, where for a few hours at a time he could live under the illusion that he was a mere "gentleman". During the last few years of his reign, after the death of the Queen, he even installed Madame Du Barry here.

Louis XVI took over this apartment for his own use and merely added some laboratories, workshops and an observatory, in accordance with his interest in the exact sciences.

The Library – Made for Madame Adélaïde in 1753 as an extension to her first-floor apartment, it was later attached to Madame Du Barry's apartment.

The Bathroom – Louis XV changed its location several times. This one dates from 1763. After 1769 it was incorporated into Madame Du Barry's apartment.

The Buffet Room – Fruit was prepared in this room, which is situated next to the dining room.

The Dining Room – For a number of years this room, which was installed in 1738, served as a winter dining room for Louis XV. A summer dining room was to be found on the floor above, and gave onto a terrace.

The Drawing Room – Originally this room and the one next to it were joined together to form the Little Gallery which was decorated with paintings of game hunting. In 1767 it was divided into two reception rooms.

Madame Du Barry's Bedroom – This is situated in the second half of what used to be the Little Gallery.

The Games Room – For some time this room served Louis XV as a dining room for his hunting suppers, after which it became Madame Du Barry's Games Room.

THE QUEEN'S APARTMENT

The apartment of Queen Marie-Thérèse was exactly symmetrical to that of the King, and also composed of seven rooms. The ceilings, like those of the King, were dedicated to the Olympian gods, but the paintings in the coving were of famous women of antiquity. Here too, the apartment was supplemented by a private apartment in the Old Palace.

The construction of the Gallery of Mirrors resulted in the loss of the two end rooms, but this was compensated by the new Guardroom at the foot of the Queen's Staircase. After the death of Queen Marie-Thérèse, her private apartment was connected to the King's.

In 1730 the bedroom was completely redecorated for Queen Marie Lesczynska in a triumph of the rococo style. The Queen also had a few private rooms behind her State Apartment set aside for her use and tastefully decorated. Here she gathered around her the group of cultivated people which formed her "circle".

These rooms were decorated once again by Marie-Antoinette, for whom Mique created a number of charming interiors freely inspired by the recent discoveries of Herculaneum and Pompeii. The Queen also modernized the Nobles Anteroom, a prelude to the upheavals, culminating in the Revolution, which prevented it from ever being completed.

Figures in gilded lead, symbolizing the marriage of Louis XIV to Marie-Thérèse of Austria. The King and Queen's monograms were removed during the Revolution and later replaced by that of Louis XVIII.

The Queen's Staircase – This was the most frequently used staircase in the whole palace since it led to the Queen's Apartment on the right, and the King's on the left.

The Guardroom – When it was installed in 1680, Noël
Coypel's paintings for the King's Audience Chamber, or
Jupiter Room, which had become the War Salon, were
transferred here.

Ceiling of the Guardroom, painted by Noël Coypel; it represents JUPITER IN HIS CHARRIOT DRAWN BY EAGLES.

Detail of the ceiling – In the corners there are figures in the dress of the time who appear to be leaning over the golden balustrade in order to catch a glimpse of the Queen's procession below.

SACRIFICE TO JUPITER by Noël Coypel.

QUEEN MARIE-ANTOINETTE AND HER CHIL-
DREN, by Elisabeth Vigée-Lebrun in 1787. ▶

MADAME ADELAÏDE by Adélaïde Labille-
Guiard in 1787.

◄ The Anteroom also known as the "Salle du Grand Couvert" for it was here that the King and Queen, together with members of the royal family, dined in the presence of their subjects.

The Nobles Anteroom – Here the Queen entertained her circle of friends and "presentations" took place. Only the ceiling dates back to Queen Marie-Thérèse; the wall decorations and the furniture were changed for Marie-Antoinette in 1785.

Ceiling of the Nobles Anteroom, by Michel Corneille, representing the god Mercury. Some of the most famous women of antiquity are painted in the coving.

Corner cupboard by Riesener and Gouthière.

97

Ceiling of the Queen's Bedroom – The gold grisaille decoration with the interwoven monograms of Louis XV and Marie Leszcynska, dates from 1735, as do François Boucher's medallions depicting THE QUEEN'S VIRTUES in camaieu.

GLORY SEIZING THE CHILDREN OF FRANCE, by Jean-François de Troy in 1734 – The artist used Veronese's style to depict the Dauphin, here aged five, and his elder sisters, Elisabeth and Henriette.

◀ The Bedroom – Three Queens and two Dauphines successively occupied this room. The panelling was made for Marie Leszcynska in 1730. The furnishings have been reconstructed to show how they looked on October 6, 1789, when Marie-Antoinette left the palace for good.

The fireplace in the Queen's Bedroom – The bust of QUEEN MARIE-ANTOINETTE, by Felix Lecomte, is dated 1783.

MARIE LESZCYNSKA, Queen of France and Navarra (1703-1768) by Jean-Marc Nattier in 1748.

Marie-Antoinette's jewel cabinet, a sumptuous piece of furniture made by the cabinet-maker Schwerdfeger in 1787. The three figures of Wisdom, Prudence and Abundance formerly held the royal crown.

An armchair from the "Cabinet de la Méridienne", made by Georges Jacob.

The Cabinet de la Méridienne – This charming boudoir was reserved for the "méridienne" or afternoon nap, hence its name. It was decorated in 1781, year of the birth of the Dauphin, which is evoked in the gilded bronze work around the glass panels of the doors.

The Library – This was arranged for Marie-Antoinette in 1772 when she was still Dauphine.

◀ Panelling from Marie-Josèphe of Saxony's Boudoir, moved to Marie-Antoinette's apartment.

Three Sèvres porcelain vases Chinese-style decoration, made in 1775 for Marie-Antoinette.

The Dauphine's Audience Chamber – The console table was made for Marie-Josèphe of Saxony and the barometer belonged to her son the Dauphin, future Louis XVI, who lived in this apartment after the death of his mother up to his coronation.

THE APARTMENTS OF THE DAUPHIN, THE DAUPHINE, AND THE MESDAMES DE FRANCE

From the start, the ground floor of the main body of the palace was one of the most important parts of Versailles, as much for its luxury as for the rank of the persons living there. Louis XIV had installed a sumptuous bath suite in the northern section, while his brother and sister-in-law, the Duke and Duchess d'Orléans occupied the southern one. In 1684, this couple handed over their apartment to their nephew, the Dauphin, known as "Monseigneur", who had it decorated in the most refined luxury to serve as a background for his collection of paintings and objets d'art.

After 1747, Louis XV altered most of the existing arrangements when he made new apartments for his son and daughter-in-law, Marie-Josèphe of Saxony, and his daughters, the Mesdames de France. On the eve of the Revolution, these apartments were among the most sumptuous and elegant in Versailles. Louis-Philippe was to destroy them almost entirely when he set up his History Museum in 1837. A recent series of renovations (1978-1986) have restored these apartments to their 1789 appearance (date at which the palace ceased to be inhabited), fixing the decoration definitively in that period.

The Dauphine's Second Anteroom – On the beautiful Pyrenees marble mantlepiece stands a bust of PHILIPPE D'ORLEANS, Regent of France (1674-1723), by Jean-Baptiste Le Moyne.

The Dauphine's Audience Chamber.

SPRING, by Jean-Baptiste Oudry (1749).

Desk with doors by Bernard Van Ryssen Burgh delivered to the Dauphine in February 1745 for her private study in Versailles.

The Dauphine's private Drawing Room – The painted woodwork in sanded varnish dates from 1749, as do the paintings above the door by J.B. Oudry, which represent the FOUR SEASONS.

The Dauphin's desk, made for him in 1745 by Bernard Van Ryssen Burgh.

The Dauphin's Library – The panelling of the study dates from 1755. The cornice is decorated with angel musicians, a reminder of the Dauphin's interests.

SEASCAPE, by Joseph Vernet – One of the four paintings over the doors in the Dauphin's Library representing the FOUR HOURS OF THE DAY, and painted in 1763.

The Dauphin's Audience Chamber – Only one section of the panelling, carved by Verberckt in 1747, has survived. The Dauphin commissioned Nattier to decorate the area above the doors with paintings of four of his sisters representing the elements. Today these paintings have been replaced with works by Natoire, which previously hung in Versailles and Marly.

Armchair, chair and foot-stool – These were among the items of furniture made by Georges Jacob in 1785 for Louis XVI's Games Room in the Palace of Saint-Cloud.

MARIE-LOUISE-THÉRÈSE-VICTOIRE OF FRANCE (Madame Victoire, 1733-1799) by Jean-Marc Nattier in 1748.

Globe on a dolphin stand – It encloses a second globe with mountains and sea beds in raised relief. The globe was made by Mantelle in 1781 at the request of Louis XVI for the education of his son.

The Dauphin's Room – The mantelpiece is decorated with marvellous bronze work by Caffiéri, and the panelling was carved by Verberckt in 1747.

Cupboard in rosewood and violet wood marquetry – The leaves of the doors are in Chinese lacquer set in a golded bronze frame. It was made by Bernard Van Ryssen Burgh and is similar to a cupboard which belonged to the Dauphine Marie-Josèphe of Saxony.

The Low Gallery – Built by Le Vau in 1669, it used to support a terrace which disappeared in 1678 during the works on the Gallery of Mirrors. Connected to the main vestibule of the Old Palace by five steps, this gallery forms the link between the Marble Courtyard and the gardens.

Painting above the door in the Dauphin's bedroom, entitled JUNO BORROWING A GIRDLE FROM VENUS, by Pierre.

Madame Victoire's Audience Chamber – The beautiful fireplace and parts of Verberckt's lovely panelling from 1763, have been conserved. The furniture was made by Tilliard in 1783 for the apartment which was occupied by the King of Sweden during his stay in Versailles.

Corner cupboard by Péridiez – This one and its pair were delivered in 1769 for this very room.

Madame Victoire's Bedroom – The bed recess is draped with chiné taffeta, reproducing the princess's "summer furnishing". Where the bed stood hangs a portrait of Madame Adélaïde by Nattier.

Madame Victoire's Drawing Room – The panels were carved by Rousseau in 1767, the commode was made by Foullet in 1768, and the chairs are dated 1770.

Detail of the panelling in Madame Victoire's Drawing Room.

MARIE-ADÉLAÏDE OF FRANCE (Madame Adélaïde, 1732-1800), by Jean-Marc Nattier in 1756.

◀ Madame Victoire's Library – This room has a mezzanine floor with an extension to the library on the lower part. A few bound books bearing Madame's coat of arms may be found in the cupboards.

◀ Madame Adélaïde's Drawing Room – Note the portraits of the Dauphin, future King Louis XVI, and the Dauphine Marie-Antoinette.

Tea set – This Sèvres porcelain tea set with "chinoiserie" decoration was delivered to Madame Adélaïde in 1775.

WINTER, by J.B. Restout – The paintings above the doors of Madame Adélaïde's Drawing Room represent the FOUR SEASONS and come from the Château de Bellevue which was her residence.

Madame Adélaïde's Bedroom – This apartment was first occupied by the Marquise de Pompadour who died in this very room in 1764, then by Marie-Josèphe of Saxony after her widowhood, and lastly by Madame Adélaïde who lived here until the Revolution.

THE DAUPHIN, son of Louis XV and brother of Madame Adélaïde, bust by Augustin Pajou.

Commode by Levasseur for the Count d'Artois, nephew of Madame Adélaïde. The candelabrum came from the Château de Bellevue, residence of the Mesdames.

Madame Adélaïde's Audience Chamber – The little organ probably belonged to Madame Adélaïde. The portrait of Elizabeth, Madame Adélaïde's older sister, is by J.M. Nattier

◀ MADAME HENRIETTE PLAYING THE VIOLA DE GAMBA by Nattier, a beautiful portrait which belonged to Madame Adélaïde.

MESDAMES VICTOIRE, SOPHIE AND LOUISE, by Drouais. This triple portrait hangs above the door in Madame Adélaïde's Audience Chamber.

115

The Small Guardroom – Here the King's guards defended the access to the King's private apartments. The steps in the background lead to the King's Staircase.

The King's Staircase – This elegant staircase led to the King's private drawing room on the first floor, and to his private apartments on the floors above.

◄ The "Hoqueton Room", named after the tunics of the provost guards who were charged with policing the palace. The trompe l'œil dates from 1672.

The Marble Vestibule – Situated at the centre of the Old Palace, it was built in 1679 in order to connect the Marble Courtyard with the gardens.

A plan of Gabriel's (1769) for converting the Marble Vestibule into a stucco library for Madame Sophie.

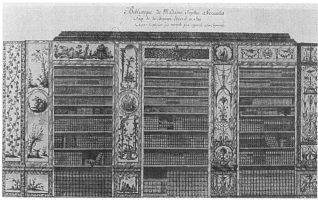

The Bathroom – The panelling depicts shells, pearls, reeds, etc. The bed comes from one of Louis XVI's "bath chambers".

LOUIS-JOSEPH-XAVIER-FRANÇOIS, DAUPHIN OF FRANCE (1781-1789) AND HIS SISTER MARIE-THÉRÈSE-CHARLOTTE (Madame Royale, 1778-1851), by Louise-Elizabeth Vigée-Lebrun in 1784.

The Bedroom of the Queen's Private Apartment.

THE ROYAL OPERA HOUSE

For a whole century the King and the Court had had to make do with temporary theatres, as often as not installed in the riding ring of the Greater Stables. Work on the present theatre was only started in 1768 and it was actually inaugurated on May 16th, 1770, on the occasion of the marriage of the Dauphin, future King Louis XVI, to the Archduchess Marie-Antoinette.

It was one of the masterpieces of the architect, Ange-Jacques Gabriel. Its original semi-oval shape, its elegant proportions, and the quality of the acoustics make this the most beautiful theatre in the world. The painter Durameau and the sculptor Pajou were given the task of decorating it, and their rich and subtle use of colour is quite worthy of the Chapel and the Gallery of Mirrors.

The huge stage was perfectly suited to the massive productions of ballets and operas, complete with nimbi, apparitions, instantaneous transformations and the large numbers of extras that were necessary to baroque opera. Moreover, as was often the case with Court theatres, the pit could be raised by a system of levers to the level of the amphitheatre and stage, thus creating another vast room suitable for a full-dress ball.

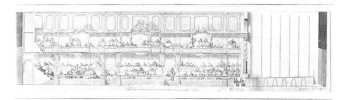

A plan by Sébastien-Antoine and Paul-Ambroise Slodtz for the theatre built in the Greater Stables on the occasion of the Dauphin's wedding on February 23, 1745.

The Opera House seen from the stage – Gabriel avoided monotony by varying the height and decoration of the four rows of boxes. The sculptures are by Pajou. The bas-reliefs of the first boxes represent the twelve principal gods of Olympus, alternating with profiles of the Muses and the Graces. The Royal Family was generally seated in the first row of the amphitheatre.

The ceiling of the Opera House – APOLLO DISTRIBUTING
CROWNS TO THE MUSES by Louis Durameau.

120

View of the stage – This is the largest one in France after the Paris Opera House. The decoration gives an idea of how the ballroom would look when, in a matter of hours the stage was converted.

The King's private box, situated in the centre of the second row of boxes. It is enclosed by gilded bronze latticework which enabled the King to attend performances without being seen.

The Foyer – Pajou decorated it with statues of APOLLO, VENUS, PACE, ABUNDANCE, YOUTH and HEALTH as well as representations of lyric, epic, pastoral and dramatic poems.

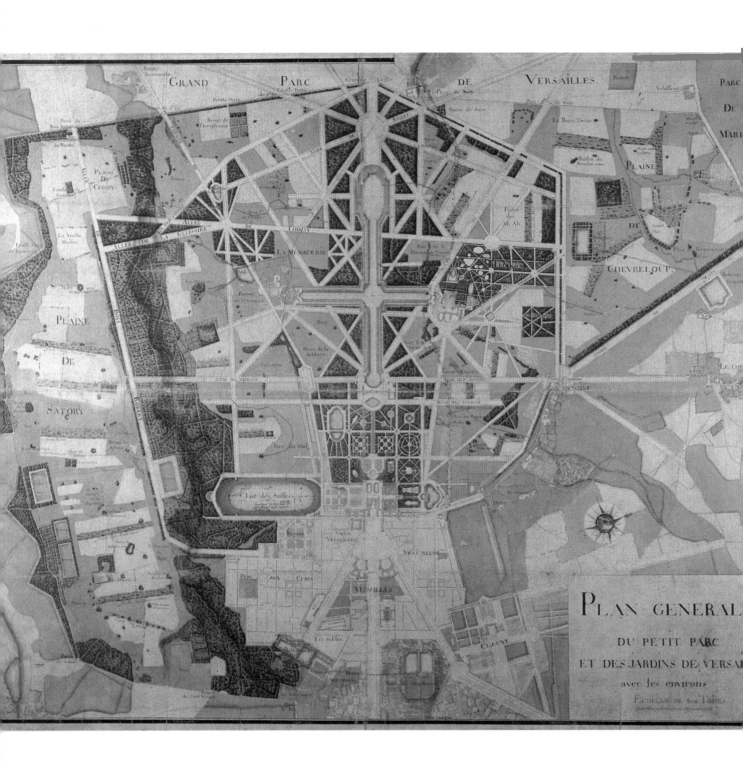

Plan of the Gardens of Versailles, drawn by Boileau in 1744.

122

THE GARDENS

The gardens, which lay in front of the west façade of the palace over some 235 acres, were laid out by André Le Nôtre. By playing on the different levels and the contrast between great perspectives and stretches of woodland hiding small groves, he created his masterpiece, and the very model of the French-style garden. Hundreds of marble and bronze statues were placed around parterres and along the tree-lined alleys, making up the largest French collection of sculptures in the round. Here too the Apollo legend provided the main theme, echoing that of the State Apartments. Thus came about an extraordinary open-air museum, reminiscent of the most famous villas of antiquity.

THE VASE OF PEACE by Tuby, in reminder of the Peace of Nijmegen which marked the apogee of Louis XIV's reign and France's supremacy in Europe.

◄ The Lakes – The edges of the two basins are decorated with bronze statues which were made by the greatest sculptors of the day and cast by the Keller brothers. They symbolize the main rivers of France and water nymphs. Their semi-reclining positions blend perfectly with the horizontal lines of the façade. Eight groups of children complete this marvellous composition, one of the most important in Versailles.

The eight statues on the following pages were part of a "great commission" in 1674, when twenty-four statues were ordered to represent the Four Elements, the Four Seasons, the Four Hours of the Day, the Four Continents, the Four Types of Poem and Man's Four Humours, in other words everything in the universe which is subject to the influence of the sun.

WATER, by Pierre Le Gros.

SPRING, by Magnier.

AIR, by Le Hongre.

DIANA, OR THE EVENING HOUR, by Martin Desjardins.

THE SEINE, by Le Hongre.

AFRICA, by Sybraique and Cornu.

WINTER, by François Girardon.

THE HEROIC POEM, by Drouilly.

THE CHOLERIC HUMOUR, by Houzeau.

THE SAONE RIVER, by Jean Baptiste Tuby.

The Water Alley – This alley and the roundabout onto which it gives are lined with twenty-two fountains from which water spurts into Languedoc marble basins supported by groups of children cast in bronze.

One of the fountains in the Water Alley, the work of Le Gros.

The Pyramid Fountain – This elegant fountain was made between 1669 and 1672 by Girardon, from a drawing by Le Brun.

◄ The Parterre of the Orangery – The Southern Parterre ends in a terrace which overlooks the Orangery Parterre, where the orange trees, pomegranates and palm trees, kept inside the Orangery during the winter months, were put out during the summer. In the background is the Swiss Lake.

Diana's Nymphs Bathing – The water from the Pyramid The Fountain falls into this basin, the main bas-relief of which is one of Girardon's masterpieces.

See page 128 :

Leto's Basin – This work of the Marsy brothers commands the entire layout of the gardens. Leto, mother of Apollo and Diana, having been insulted by the Lycian peasants, implores Jupiter to avenge her and he obliges her by transforming her persecutors into lizards and toads.
The Basin of Flora or Spring, by Tuby.
The Basin of Bacchus or Autumn, by Marsy.
▼

See page 129 :

Apollo's Charriot, by Jean-Baptiste Tuby – The god of the son driving a quadriga, emerges from the water at the start of his race across the firmament before alighting to rest in Thetis' grotto in the evening.
The Basin of Ceres or Summer, by Regnaudin.
The Basin of Saturn or Winter, by Girardon.

BACCHANTE, by Dedieu, one of the most beautiful terminal statues bordering Leto's Parterre.

The Isle of Children – This charming fountain was designed by Hardy in 1710, with gilded lead figures originally from the Porcelain Trianon. ▼

The Labyrinth Grove – This painting by Cotelle depicts the entrance to a grove which contained thirty-nine fountains decorated with groups of animals depicting Aesop's Fables. This grove was destroyed during the reign of Louis XVI.

◄ Ornamental Fountains, by Cotelle – This grove, despite its ephemeral existance, was one of the most entrancing with its patterns of greenery and variety of fountains.

The Colonnade Grove – Hardouin-Mansart designed this circular peristyle, thirty-two meters in diameter, with columns in different kinds of marble supporting white marble arcades. The decoration in the spandrels represents children's games. ▼

The Ballroom Grove – Le Nôtre used the incline of the ground for his cascades of water which partly veiled the grotto. A marble platform stood in the centre of the grove for the dancers.

Apollo's Bath Grove – This was created in 1778 from a project by Hubert Robert to provide a setting for the marble figures made a century earlier for Thetis' Grotto, entitled APOLLO WAITED ON BY THE NYMPHS OF THETIS, by Girardon and Regnaudin, and TRITONS LOOKING AFER THE HORSES OF THE SUN, by Marsy and Gilles Guérin.

THE TRIANON PALACE, by Pierre-Denis Martin in 1722 – The
roof balustrade used to be decorated with sculptures which
have since disappeared.

THE TRIANON

This little palace was built by Jules Hardouin-Mansart in place of the "Porcelain Trianon" which Le Vau had erected in 1670.

It is a one-storey building, its flat roof hidden behind a balustrade on which originally stood a number of sculptures of children and baskets of flowers, but these unfortunately disappeared during the 19th century. The façades are rythmically punctuated with ionic pilasters of Languedoc marble and fine decorations are carved around the French windows, the same motifs of intertwined flowers and musical instruments which can be found inside the palace. The two wings are connected by a peristyle, through which may be glimpsed the garden beyond, and the front of which is embellished by eight mottled Campan marble columns, arranged in pairs.

Louis XIV liked to spend warm summer evenings here, and he occasionaly spent the night, but only with members of the royal family. Louis XV showed no interest in the palace in the early part of his reign. He gave it to the Queen who used it to entertain her father, the former King of Poland, Stanislas Leszczynski, when he visited her. Nevertheless, in 1750 Louis XV installed a new apartment there which he occupied from time to time until the Little Trianon was built.

The palace was stripped of its furniture and works of art by the Revolution. In 1805 Napoleon restored it and refurnished it in order to house his mother, who refused to move in. After 1810 the Emperor occasionally stayed in the palace for a few days at a time, in the company of his second wife, Empress Marie-Louise. Louis XVIII and Charles X only visited the place briefly, but Louis-Philippe frequently gathered his vast family there, thus renewing with a tradition which had been interrupted since the death of Louis XIV.

Today the Trianon palace has been renovated and is used for entertaining visiting heads of state.

A sunk fence, bordered with balustrades, separates the forecourt of the main courtyard, which is enclosed with a railing decorated with fleurs-de-lys.

Pages 134-135 :
The Trianon façade overlooking the parterres–Its long horizontal lines are broken up by the projection of the peristyle and the end pavillions. In the foreground can be seen the ramp of the perron leading to the Garden Salon.

The Peristyle – Louis XIV himself designed this elegant "loggia" and gave it its name. On summer evenings he liked to dine here. The angle wing houses the Gallery and the Garden Salon.

Façade of the wing of Trianon-sous-Bois by Jules Hardouin. Mansart in 1705.

◄ Tiered Fountain – This marble fountain was built by Hardouin-Mansart in 1703, but the statues of Neptune and Amphitrite, the bas-relief of the Triumph of Thetis as well as the other sculptures were the works of a number of artists including Van Clève and Claude Lorrain.

The Empress' First Drawing Room – This was formerly the anteroom to Louis XIV's Chapel. The furniture was made for Empress Marie-Louise.

Detail of the panelling – The Apollo's head and the fleurs-delys are a reminder that the decoration of this room was intended for Louis XIV in 1700.

The Empress' Bedroom, which formerly belonged to Louis XIV, and then the Dauphin.

The Mirror Room – The decoration dates from Louis XIV ▶ who used this room as an Audience Chamber. Marie-Louise had it converted into her study.

SAINT JOHN THE EVANGELIST, by Charles Le Brun.

The Empress' Boudoir – Note the beautiful "arc de triomphe" desk made for Madame Bonaparte, the future Empress Josephine, by the Jacob brothers.

▲ The Round Salon – Its attractive decoration of corinthian colums was completed during the reign of Louis XV by two revolving doors, the right-hand one containing a tiny chapel.

The Officers' Anteroom, used as a dining room by Louis XIV. ▼

▲ The Grand Reception Room – Under Louis-Philippe, the royal family used to gather in this vast room in the evenings. The King had made it by knocking down the wall separating the Senior Officers' Anteroom and the Princes' Salon.

The Emperor's Audience Chamber–The malachites given to Napoleon by the Czar Alexander 1st, were mounted in bronze by Thomire. ▼

The Cool Dining Room – This pavillion, which is quite symmetrical to the Menagerie in relation to the French Pavillion, was used as a summer dining room.

The Garden Salon – This opens onto a quincunx and the parterres. Under Louis XIV a special porch game was played here, and during the Empire it housed a billiard table.

The Gallery, decorated with paintings by Jean Cotelle dated 1688 and representing the parterres and the groves of Versailles and Trianon.

◀ Ebony and gilded bronze console dresser with malachite top by Jacob Desmalter in 1809.

The Springhead Salon – This opened onto the grove from which it derived its name and which disappeared under Louis XVI. Napoleon used this room for charting maps.

The Anteroom of the Emperor's Private Apartment – This occupies part of the former Audience Chamber of the Marquise de Maintenon.

The Emperor's Private Drawing Room, formerly Madame de Maintenon's bedroom.

The Emperor's Bedroom – This used to be Louis XV's bedroom and was redecorated in December 1809 for Napoleon.

Commode by Baudoin and wall hangings in buff-coloured watered-silk with a lilac and silver brocade border.

The Breakfast Room, where Napoleon would take his first meal of the day.

The Emperor's Family Drawing Room – This was formerly Louis XV's Games Room. The fireplace and the panelling were placed there in 1750.

The Dining Room – This was made in 1750 by joining Louis XIV's last bedroom and his private drawing room. Much of the panelling dates from 1703.

The French Garden Pavillion – Built by Gabriel in 1750 in
the heart of the garden from which it gets its name, this is
one of the most charming examples of the rococo style.

144

THE LITTLE TRIANON

This charming estate was Louis XV's creation. Passionately interested by botany, he planted a botanical garden and placed Jussieu in charge of it, enabling him to apply his new plant classification system for the first time.

Along with the botanical garden, which included a number of hot houses, was a French-style garden in the middle of which stood an elegant pavillion for rest and conversation, a summer dining area, and a small menagerie where domestic animals were reared and selected.

In 1764, the King asked Gabriel to build a little palace between the two gardens, to enable him to stay for short spells near the garden he liked so much. This became the "Little Trianon", to distinguish it from Louis XIV's pink marble palace, and its harmonious proportions and exquisite decoration make it an undisputed masterpiece of neo-classical architecture. Louis XVI gave this estate to Marie-Antoinette and it became her favourite abode, one in which she could lead a simple family life with her children and a few friends, reminiscent of her Viennese childhood. She removed Louis XV's botanical garden and replaced it with an Anglo-Chinese one according to the taste of the day. It was in this enchanting place that she was to be found on October 5th, 1789, when a page came to announce that the Parisians were marching on Versailles. The Queen left her beloved Trianon post-haste, little thinking that she would never return.

The Central Salon of the French Pavillion – The panelling by Verberckt depicts hunting, fishing and gardening, while the frieze represents domestic animals.

The Little Trianon seen from the French Garden side – With its avant-corps of corinthian columns and the stairs leading to the parterre, this is a particularly harmonious façade.

The Staircase – The sober stones are discreetly highlighted by the richness of the gilded wrought-iron railings.

The Dining Room – The fruit motifs of the woodwork and the mantelpiece are a reminder of the room's purpose, as are the subjects of the paintings.   Here Louis XV and, later, Marie-Antoinette gave their supper parties.

FISHING, by Doyen – This beautiful painting and the three other ones hanging in the dining room, HUNTING, THE HARVEST and GRAPE PICKING, depict the principal sources of our foodstuffs.

The Little Dining Room – Marie-Antoinette turned this into a billiard room.

147

The Drawing Room – Flowers are the principal motif in the panelling while the paintings over the doors represent themes from Ovid's *Metamorphoses*. Note the beautiful lamp in gilded bronze and blued steel.

The Queen's Bedroom, formerly Louis XV's private drawing room – Marie-Antoinette decorated it with carved wooden furniture, realistically painted, and covered with embroidered material with a wild flower motif.

The Boudoir – The delicate woodwork was designed by Mique and the furniture used to belong to the Comte de Provence, brother-in-law of Marie-Antoinette.

148

The Queen's Theatre – This was built in 1780 by Richard Mique. Although the auditorium is fairly small, as befits a private theatre, the stage is large enough to set full scale operas.

Inside Belvedere – A beautiful marble mosaic covers the floor and the walls are decorated with fine arabesques by Le Riche.

Pages 150-151:

The Rock Pavillion, or Belvedere – This charming octagonal pavillion overlooks the little lake. The bas-reliefs of the windows represent the seasons, while the door pediments are decorated with hunting and gardening emblems.

The Temple of Love – This elegant construction of Mique's, dated 1778, houses an ancient copy of Bouchardon's statue LOVE TRIMMING HIS ARC FROM HERCULES' BLUDGEON.

MARCUS CURTIUS – This was first an equestrian statue of
Louis XIV, made by Lorenzo Bernini between 1665 and
1680. When it arrived in Versailles it was transformed into
Marcus Curtius by Girardon and placed at the far end of the
Swiss Lake. Today it has been replaced with a copy.

THE GREATER STABLES

The Greater Stables (Grande Écurie) were built by Jules Hardouin-Mansart between 1679 and 1682. The Master of the Horse was housed there, along with the numerous staff under him: equerries, pages, chaplains, tutors to the pages, grooms, saddlers, etc.

During the 19th-century the stables were converted into a barracks and today the site is shared by a number of government departments. The pages' chapel and the four galleries which formerly housed the horses are now part of a museum. In the southern section 18th-century sleighs and sedan chairs are exhibited, as well as a dozen 19th-century carriages, including the one used by Charles X on his coronation. The northern section of the museum has a number of beautiful statues on display, originally from the gardens of Versailles, now replaced by copies, together with a few decorations from the long-gone groves.

Spandrel of the main door – The leaping steeds are the work of Raon and Garnier.

PERSEPHONE'S ABDUCTION BY HADES – This masterpiece of Girardon's was part of a commission of four groups to symbolize the Four Elements, only three of which were completed; Louis XIV had placed this one at the centre of the Colonade Grove.

One of the sculpture galleries which houses various decorative items from the former groves, including the polychrome lead figures which formerly decorated the fountains in the Labyrinth Grove.

The Carriage Gallery – This houses the 18th-century sleighs and sedan chairs, as well as a dozen coaches, the oldest of which dates back to Napoleon's wedding to the Archduchess Marie-Louise.

The coronation carriage – Made from drawings by Percier for Charles X's coronation (May 29, 1825), it was unfortunately altered for the baptism of the Imperial Prince in 1856.